Starlight and Time

Solving the Puzzle of Distant Starlight in a Young Universe

D. Russell Humphreys, Ph.D.

Master Books
Colorado Springs, Colorado

Copyright © 1994 Master Books

Second printing: June 1995

Creation-Life Publishers, Inc.
Master Books
P.O. Box 26060
Colorado Springs, CO 80936
(719) 591-0800

ISBN: 0-89051-202-7

Library of Congress Catalog Card Number: 94-79857

Cover art: Ron Hight

Table of Contents

About the Author

D. Russell Humphreys, B.S., Ph.D.

Dr. Humphreys was awarded his Ph.D. in physics from Louisiana State University in 1972, by which time he was a fully convinced creationist. For the next 6 years he worked in the High Voltage Laboratory of General Electric Company, designing and inventing equipment and researching high-voltage phenomena. While there, he received a U.S. patent and one of *Industrial Research Magazine's* IR-100 awards. Since 1979 he has worked for Sandia National Laboratories in nuclear physics, geophysics, pulsed-power research, and theoretical atomic and nuclear physics. Since 1985 he has been working with Sandia's Particle Beam Fusion Project, and was co-inventor of special laser-triggered "Rimfire" high-voltage switches, now coming into wider use.

The last few years have seen a greater emphasis on theoretical nuclear physics and radiation hydrodynamics in an effort to help produce the world's first lab-scale thermonuclear fusion. He has published some 20 papers in secular scientific journals, as well as many creationist technical papers. Besides gaining another US patent, he has been given two awards from Sandia, including an Award for Excellence for contributions to light ion-fusion target theory. Dr. Humphreys is an adjunct professor of the Institute for Creation Research in San Diego, a board member of the Creation Research Society, and is president of the Creation Science Fellowship of New Mexico.

About this Book

The bulk of the text was initially produced as a chapter intended for a forthcoming book for the non-technical reader, explaining many of the evidences for a young age for the earth and universe. The book is to be called *Thousands, not Billions: Exciting, Easy-to-Understand Evidence for a Young World*. This eagerly-anticipated project is, despite Dr. Humphreys' busy research schedule, close to being finalized, with publication expected by early 1996.

However, the issue of starlight travel-time is so important (and is seen by so many as an immovable stumbling block to the Christian faith) that it was felt there was a certain urgency about expanding this chapter into a separate book in the meantime.

Dr. Humphreys' collaborator in these writing projects (not including the reprinted technical papers) is Dr. Carl Wieland, Managing Director of the Creation Science Foundation Ltd. of Australia.

Foreword by Ken Ham

I have been actively involved in the creation ministry for over 15 years, having visited many different countries and spoken to hundreds of thousands of people. I have also had the unique opportunity of mixing with the world's leading creation scientists, observing them admirably defend Genesis creation despite the probing attacks of antagonistic evolutionists.

Creationist research has exposed many of the weaknesses and flaws in evolutionary philosophy, and has provided answers in such areas as geology and biology. These contributions have given public speakers such as myself a good degree of confidence to give "reasons for what we believe" when challenged by opponents.

However, if I were asked whether there were any major places of weakness in the creationist armor, I would have to admit that it has been (till now at least) in the area of cosmology.

One of the most-asked questions directed to me at our seminars and through the mail goes something like this: "If the universe is only thousands of years old, how do you explain the millions of years it takes for light to travel from distant stars?"

I have heard creation scientists attempt to solve this seemingly insurmountable problem for those who believe the Bible's account of a young world. However, until I read Dr. Russ Humphreys' new creationist cosmology as outlined in this book, I was not convinced of real progress towards a complete, scientifically satisfying framework.

How exciting it is to see in this book such a God-honoring approach in a scientific discipline that has involved meticulous work (by a scientist well qualified in his field, with review by qualified peers) in this area of front-line importance in the "battle for the Bible." Some traditional creationist concepts will be challenged as you read this, but we need to remember that scientific theories and models are always subject to change—the Word of God is not.

Your heart will be warmed as you learn of viable answers to those within and without the Christian camp who would challenge a real six-day creation because of Big Bang theories and the starlight questions.

Ken Ham, B.App.Sc., Dip. Ed.

Answers in Genesis
Florence, Kentucky

Chapter 1

Solving the "Unsolvable Problem"

Whenever I have spoken on the positive physical evidences for a recent creation, an extremely common question which many people ask is this: "If the universe is so young, how can we see light from stars that are more than 10,000 light-years away?" A light-year is the distance that light travels at its present speed in one year, about ten trillion kilometers.

For example, consider the most frequently observable very distant objects that astronomers can see in the sky—galaxies. Galaxies are large clusters of stars, typically 100 billion or so, roughly 100,000 light-years in diameter. There are about 100 billion galaxies within the viewing range of our best telescopes. The galaxy we are a part of, the Milky Way, is a very typical galaxy.

A relatively close neighboring galaxy, M31 in Andromeda, is supposed to be so distant that light traveling at today's speed would take about two million years to reach us. At that speed, if the universe were only six to ten thousand years old, the first light from the Andromeda galaxy could hardly have traveled more than a few percent of its way toward earth. Yet stargazers in the northern hemisphere can see it with binoculars.

In the southern hemisphere, people can see our nearest neighbor galaxies, the two Magellanic clouds, with the naked eye. Yet they are supposed to be on the order of 100,000 light years away. The most distant galaxy astronomers have observed to date is supposed to be about 12 billion light-years away. If the universe is young, people ask, how can we be seeing the light from such distant objects?

Some laymen pondering this question wonder if the astronomers' estimates of distances might be greatly in error. I don't think so. Astronomers have dozens of methods for estimating such distances, all of which generally agree with one another. Many of the methods, especially for closer objects such as the Andromeda galaxy, are based on very reasonable assumptions, such as the overall size or brightness of a galaxy.

For that reason, I am convinced that the large distances are generally correct, at least within a factor of two or so. Certainly, it is hard to imagine how correcting errors in all these methods could somehow shrink, say, the twelve billion light-years mentioned above down to ten thousand light-years. Thus, the question represents a problem which is very real and needs to be answered.

Because of the testimony of Scripture and the weight of other evidence favoring a recent creation, young-earth creationists have tried a number of theories to explain how the light from distant galaxies got here in less than 10,000 years. These have thus far not been very successful (Appendix A). Since 1985 I have been working on a new theory to explain this problem and other large-scale phenomena in the cosmos, such as red shifts in the light from distant galaxies and the cosmic microwave background radiation (Appendix C).

Two papers of mine on this new young-earth creationist cosmology (an alternative to the Big Bang) have had very positive peer review at the Third International Conference on Creationism (ICC). They are reprinted in Appendices B and C for those readers wanting more technical details. Cosmology is a very complex and subtle subject, but I will try to strip it down to the bare essentials here.

Gravity Distorts Time

Let me first briefly outline where I am heading. The theory utilizes Einstein's general theory of relativity, which is the best theory of gravity we have today. General relativity (GR) has been well-established experimentally, and is the physics framework for all modern cosmologies. According to GR, *gravity affects time*. Clocks at a low altitude should tick more slowly than clocks at a high altitude—and observations confirm this effect, which some call *gravitational time dilation*. (Not to be confused with the better-known "velocity" time dilation in Einstein's special relativity theory.)

For example, an atomic clock at the Royal Observatory in Greenwich, England, ticks five microseconds per year slower than an identical clock at the National Bureau of Standards in Boulder, Colorado, both clocks being accurate to about one microsecond per year. The difference is exactly what general relativity predicts for the one-mile difference in altitude (Figure 1).

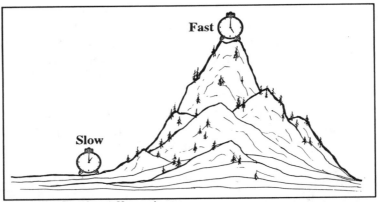

Figure 1 Gravity Affects time.

Which one is showing (or running at) the "right time"? Both are—in their own frame of reference. There is no longer any way to say which is the "correct" rate at which time runs—it all depends on where you are in relation to a gravitational field. A large variety of more precise experiments has confirmed gravitational time dilation to an accuracy of better than one percent—it's for real!

The effect applies to the rates of *all* physical processes—the earth rotating beneath your feet, decay of atomic nuclei in your bones, how fast you get old, the ticking of the watch on your wrist, and the speed of nerve impulses in your brain. This means that locally, the effect is unnoticeable. Whatever measurements were made at one altitude would not show the effect, because everything at that altitude would be slowed by the same factor. You would have to compare clocks at different altitudes to see a difference.

Six Real Earth-days

What this new cosmology shows is that gravitational time distortion in the early universe would have meant that while a few days were passing on earth, billions of years would have been available for light to travel to earth. It still means that God made the heavens and earth (i.e., the whole universe) in six ordinary days, only a few thousand years ago. But with the reality revealed by GR, we now know that we have to ask—six days as measured by *which clock*? In which frame of reference? The mathematics of this new theory shows that while God makes the universe in six days *in the earth's reference frame* ("Earth Standard Time," if you like), the light has ample time *in the extra-terrestrial reference frame* to travel the required distances.

None of these timeframes can be said to be "God's time" since the Creator, who sees the end from the beginning (Isaiah 46:10, Rev. 22:13, John 8:58, and more) is outside of time. Time is a created feature of His universe, like matter and space. It is interesting that the equations of GR have long indicated that time itself had a beginning.

It might be suspected that such a startling result requires some fairly creative manipulation, but interestingly, the result "falls out" of the equations of GR (the same mathematical machinery used to

generate the Big Bang theory), just as does the Big
Bang. The crucial reason why such different
cosmologies come out of the same mathematics is
that two different (but absolutely arbitrary) starting
points (initial assumptions) are utilized, as we will
see. We need to understand more about Big Bang
theory to be able to understand this creationist
alternative.

What the Big Bang Theorists Fail to Tell You

Most non-experts (in fact, most scientists not trained
in cosmology) are unaware that the universe assumed
by the Big Bang theorist has no boundaries, no edge
and no center. Most people visualize the Big Bang as
shown in Figure 2a, like a ball of matter expanding
into space—but that would imply that it had
boundaries, and that's not how the experts see it.
They prefer to assume that there is *no edge* to the
three-dimensional space we live in—or to the matter
therein (figure 2b). (See, for example, the well-known
undergraduate text by cosmologist Edward R.
Harrison, *Cosmology: The Science of the Universe*,
Cambridge University Press, 1981, especially
pp. 106–107.)

There are basically two versions of Big-Bang
cosmology. The most popular one is the *finite* form,
which maintains that if you traveled in space far
enough, though you wouldn't ever reach the edge
(there is none), you could (if you could travel fast
enough) end up coming right back to your starting
point. Imagine an ant crawling on the surface of a

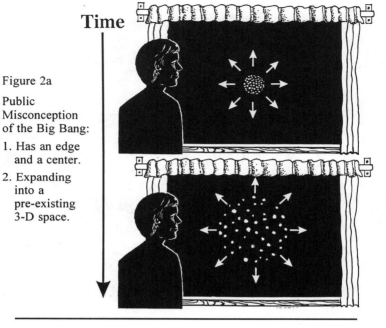

Figure 2a

Public
Misconception
of the Big Bang:

1. Has an edge
   and a center.

2. Expanding
   into a
   pre-existing
   3-D space.

Figure 2b

Expert's
Conception of
the Big Bang:

1. No edge and
   no center.

2. 3-D space
   expands
   with matter.

balloon—it never reaches the edge of its two-dimensional space—there is none! But this space is nevertheless not infinitely large, and the ant could end up at its starting point just by traveling in a straight line.

Figure 3   Imagining Our Universe as the Surface of a Balloon

Now imagine sequins (representing galaxies, for instance) pasted on and uniformly spotting the surface of the balloon. As the balloon expands in three dimensions, so this two-dimensional space on its surface stretches and causes each sequin to move away from every other sequin. Now hang onto your hats, because it's really impossible for anyone to actually imagine a fourth dimension, but the equations of GR seem to require that space have an extra dimension. (One more than length, breadth, and width—and I'm not referring to *time* as the extra dimension). To understand a little more of what the Big Bang theory is saying, we have to move our sequin/balloon example up by one dimension, as follows.

We've seen that the three-dimensional (3-D) expansion of the balloon causes the "galaxies" to move apart in 2-D. Just so, the Big Bang proposes that our 3-D space is on the "surface" of a four-dimensional (4-D) sphere which is undergoing a 4-D expansion. The resultant effect is to cause galaxies to move away from all other galaxies in 3-D space.

	Sequins/Balloon		**Big Bang Theory**
Expansion in:	3 Dimensions	➡	4 Dimensions
Stretching of:	2-Dimensional Space	➡	3-Dimensional Space
Objects move away from each other in:	2 Dimensions	➡	3 Dimensions

Step up one Dimension

There is no "center" to this proposed expansion, just as, on the surface of the balloon, there is no central point from which all other sequins are receding. On the balloon, the sequins which begin furthest away from each other are moving apart more rapidly. This is given as the reason that the further a galaxy is from earth, the faster it appears to be moving away from us. The shift of its light to the red end of the spectrum is interpreted as a measure of its speed, although Appendix C explains that such a "Doppler effect" is not really what general relativists think is the cause of such "redshifting."

Incidentally, this hopefully explains an aspect of Big Bang theory many non-experts find puzzling. If, they say, distant galaxies are all believed to be moving away from us, then surely that means we're supposed to be in the center of the "bang"? The answer, as we have seen, is that in Big-Bang theory, somebody on one of those distant galaxies also sees the same sort of redshift pattern we do, and would be able to interpret this as if distant galaxies were receding from that point. (Because every galaxy is supposed to be moving away from every other galaxy in three dimensions.)

In the *infinite* versions of the Big Bang, by the way, it is assumed that matter and space are infinite—you would just keep traveling forever and come across more and more space and matter. The space is expanding, but across an infinite vista. According to these theories, if you went traveling in the early universe, you would find matter to be more dense and very hot, but again you could travel forever and would never come to a region where there was no matter.

Why No Boundary?

Why do Big-Bang cosmologists use as their starting point the assumption (which seems quite contrary to common sense) that the universe has no boundary? Is there some good scientific reason, or is it perhaps demanded or even suggested by well-established, experimentally-backed theory, like general relativity?

The answer is no. It is an *arbitrary assumption,* called the "cosmological principle," or more recently the "Copernican principle." This assumes that (whether the universe is finite—like that of the ant on the balloon—or infinite) there is no edge and no center. On a large enough scale, matter is evenly distributed around us. Therefore, it is asked, if there were an edge, then why don't we see more galaxies on one side of us than on the other?

This would be easy to explain if we were in a special place close to the center. Such a "special arrangement" is exceedingly improbable on a chance basis. It therefore strongly smacks of purpose, and is thus unpalatable to most theorists today, who prefer to believe in a universe ruled by randomness. So it is simply assumed that there *is* no center, and no boundary. In this assumption, every part of the universe will appear to have matter evenly distributed around it as well.

It may not be unfair to suggest another possible reason for the near-universal acceptance of this assumption. To allow the possibility of anything "outside" the universe (perhaps God?) makes it harder to hold the position that the universe is "all there is" (the popular position of philosophical materialism).

Why have I spent so much time on this belief in an unbounded universe? In such a universe, every galaxy is surrounded by an even distribution of other galaxies, and there is no net gravitational force (on a large enough scale). However, if the universe is bounded, then there would be a center of mass and a net gravitational force, and we could begin to consider the time-distorting effects of gravity on a massive scale.

In such a universe, clocks at the edge of the universe would be ticking at a rate different from clocks at the center. However, this effect, though significant, would be nowhere near enough to give the huge time dilation mentioned.

Returning to the "unbounded" assumption: when this is fed into the "hopper" of general relativity (Figure 4), the Big-Bang cosmology "falls out"—it is a natural consequence of the equations. Actually, two options fall out: either things are expanding from a Big Bang or they are collapsing into a Big Crunch. The choice between the two is made on the basis of observations which certainly indicate that things are

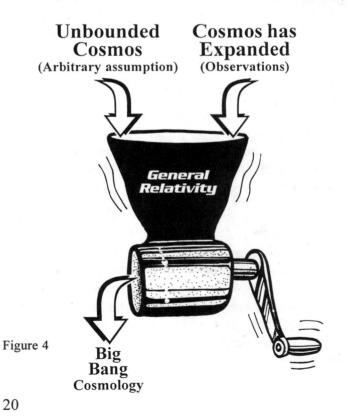

Unbounded Cosmos
(Arbitrary assumption)

Cosmos has Expanded
(Observations)

General Relativity

Figure 4

Big Bang Cosmology

not collapsing. In fact, there is sound observational evidence that the universe has expanded.

However, what if we begin our calculations with the opposite assumption, equally scientifically valid, namely that matter in the universe *has* a center and an edge (is bounded)? This makes more common sense and is also Scripturally far more appropriate. When we feed in this, plus the same observations, into general relativity, quite a different cosmology falls out.

I call it a "White Hole" cosmology for reasons to become clearer shortly—and it just happens to solve the problem of the starlight travel-time rather neatly.

Expansion Affects the Time Difference

For a given amount of matter, the bigger the radius in which it is contained, the less the effect of gravitational time dilation. If we assume that the matter we can observe with telescopes is all there is (i.e., the edge of matter is closer than, say, 20 billion light-years), then our clocks are ticking only a few percent slower than clocks near the edge. This is not enough to solve the problem.

However, when I referred to this new cosmology as "falling out," I mentioned that *observations* had to be fed into the "hopper" as well. After many years of studying the evidence, I am convinced that the observations indicate that the universe has indeed expanded significantly, by a factor of at least one thousand (Appendix C).

There also appears to be Scriptural evidence for such an expansion; for example, the following verse:

Who stretches out the heavens like a curtain, and spreads them out like a tent to dwell in. Isaiah 40:22

My exegetical ICC article lists seventeen such verses throughout the Old Testament (see reprint in Appendix B). The verses use four different Hebrew verbs and occur in a wide variety of contexts. Their frequency and diversity suggested to me as far back as 1985 that they might not be mere metaphors. Instead, they could be referring to the same expansion of space permitted in GR and used in many cosmologies.

Thus, there seem to be both Biblical and scientific reasons for thinking the universe was much smaller in the past. In a bounded universe, some startling effects would then occur.

Black Holes and Event Horizons

Imagine this bounded universe when it was about fifty times smaller than today (see page 107). The equations of GR would then allow the universe to be in one of two states (no other states are possible). One of the possibilities (we will shortly discuss the other) is that the whole universe would be inside a huge *black hole.*

Black holes are more than just theoretical concepts. They are, first, direct predictions of general relativity, which is backed by a great deal of experimental evidence. In addition, most astronomers are convinced they have observational evidence of possibly three star-sized black holes, and very strong evidence for another one, millions of times larger. As huge quantities of matter fall towards such black holes, copious amounts of energy are given off. The giant one, recently discovered, is at the center of the galaxy M87; astronomers know of no cause other than a black hole to explain what they observe.

Black holes can be very small or very large—it all depends on the amount of matter packed within a given radius. The combined gravitational force of all the mass inside a black hole is so strong that light rays cannot escape—hence the name.

This means that all the matter within our fifty-times-smaller universe would have been trapped within an intangible spherical border called the *event horizon,* at least a billion light-years in diameter. This is the point at which light rays trying to escape a black hole bend back on themselves; it is also where time is massively distorted.

The diameter of an event horizon depends on the amount of matter inside it. This means that the event horizon of, say, a star-sized black hole, the gravity of which causes it to swallow more and more matter, will increase—like a fat man gorging himself and growing ever fatter.

Matter and light can exist inside a black hole; however, the equations of GR require that they must fall inward, eventually reaching the "singularity" at the center, where they would be crushed down to a pinpoint of nearly infinite density. However, as mentioned, the evidence indicates that the universe has expanded and is not currently undergoing such an overall inward-falling. Therefore the universe cannot now be within a black hole.

White Holes

Given a bounded universe that was once fifty times smaller, the other possibility allowed by GR is that the universe was previously in a huge *white hole*. This is a black hole running in reverse. Astrophysicists of the 1970's gave that name to the concept, arising from theoretical studies of black holes. The name never really became popular, but the concept is still considered valid today.

Like a black hole, a white hole would also have an event horizon. Matter and light could exist inside its event horizon without any particular problems. There need be no singularity at its center, except perhaps at the very beginning of its existence. However, the equations of GR require that light and matter inside the event horizon of a white hole must expand outward.

The event horizon of a white hole would be a one-way border which permits only *outward motion* through itself. Matter and light waves would have to move out of a white hole, but they could not go back in. Since the diameter of an event horizon is proportional to the amount of matter inside it, the event horizon would shrink as matter passes through it and out of the white hole. The analogy would be a fat man on a very strict diet—no input allowed, only output! Eventually, he would waste away. In the same way, the event horizon would get smaller and smaller, and eventually shrink to nothing. There would then be no more white hole, but only scattered matter moving away from a central point.

Some Scientific Conclusions

Remember, I did not invent these seemingly strange ideas about black and white holes. Instead, they are a consequence of the best knowledge we have today about gravity. The equations of GR permit, but do not demand, the existence of white holes today.

We see, therefore, from this discussion (and Appendix C) that, just by starting with the assumption that the universe is bounded (and accepting the overwhelming observational evidence that it has expanded), the following deductive sequence applies.

1. *The visible universe was once inside an event horizon.*

   This means it was once either within a black hole or a white hole. We have seen that if it were a black hole, it would be contracting, which is not indicated by the evidence. Therefore:

2. *The visible universe was once inside a white hole.*

   It may, however, have commenced as a black hole before expansion started—Appendix C. If the universe is not much bigger or much denser than what we can directly observe right now (see Appendix C for other possibilities), then calculations in Appendix C show that an event horizon can no longer exist. This means that the event horizon has shrunk to zero radius sometime in the past, meaning that an expansion of space continued at least until the white hole ceased to exist.

So from all the physics and astronomical data we now know, we can draw a straightforward conclusion:

If the universe is bounded, then sometime in its past the universe must have expanded out of a white hole.

An unbounded universe (such as a Big-Bang cosmos) could never be in a black or white hole at any time in its history, because there would be no center in 3-D

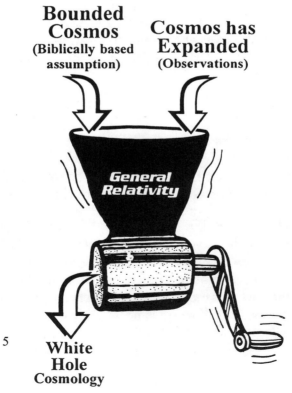

Bounded Cosmos
(Biblically based assumption)

Cosmos has Expanded
(Observations)

General Relativity

Figure 5

White Hole
Cosmology

space for gravitational forces to point to. Thus, unbounded and bounded cosmologies are profoundly different. Both types of cosmology are equally rigorous deductions from their starting assumptions. Compare Figure 4 (page 20) with Figure 5.

So the main scientific question is this: which input-assumption gives a better explanation of the cosmos we live in? The following sections show how the White Hole cosmology can explain the same data as the Big Bang, while retaining the idea of a young earth. But more than that, the White Hole cosmology seems to have a very good chance of explaining data which the Big Bang cannot (Appendix C).

Event Horizons and Time

Strange things happen to time near an event horizon. In his popular book *A Brief History of Time* (Bantam Books, 1988, p. 87), Stephen Hawking tells the story of a man, say an astronaut, falling toward the event horizon of a black hole. I paraphrase it here as follows:

> The astronaut is scheduled to reach the event horizon at 12:00 noon, as measured by his watch. As he falls toward it, a dark sphere blocking off the starry background, an astronomer watching him from far away sees that the astronaut's watch is ticking slower and slower. By the astronomer's wall clock, it takes an hour for the astronaut's watch to go from 11:57 am to 11:58. And then *a day* to reach 11:59! The astronomer never does see the astronaut's watch reach 12:00. Instead, he sees

the motionless images of the astronaut and his watch getting redder and dimmer, finally fading from view completely.

Hawking didn't describe much of what *the astronaut* could see, so here I take up his story:

As the astronaut approaches the event horizon, he looks back through binoculars at the astronomer's wall clock and sees it running faster and faster. He sees the astronomer moving rapidly around the laboratory like a video in fast-forward. He sees planets and stars moving very rapidly in their orbits. The whole universe far away from him is moving at a frenzied pace, aging rapidly. Yet the astronaut sees that his own watch is ticking normally. When his watch reaches 12:00 noon, the astronaut sees the hands of the astronomer's wall clock moving forward so fast they are just a blur. As he crosses the event horizon, he feels no particular sensation, but now he sees bright light *inside* the horizon. His watch reaches 12:01 and continues ticking.

The main point is that according to GR, *time effectively stands still at the event horizon.* Clocks and all physical processes at that location are stopped, and near that location they run very slowly (relative to clocks away from it). We have already shown how the scientific evidence indicates that the universe (with the earth roughly at its center) must have expanded out of a white hole which no longer exists. This means that the event horizon shrank down to zero. (GR sets no limit on the speed at which such a shrinkage can take place, incidentally.)

If you were standing on the earth as the event horizon arrived, distant objects in the universe could age billions of years in a single day of your time. And there would be ample time for their light to reach you.

What Is the Biblical Time Standard?

In a bounded universe, clocks in different places can tick (or register time) at drastically different rates. So which set of clocks is the Bible referring to in Genesis 1, or in Exodus 20:11, when it says that God made the universe in six ordinary weekdays? In Appendix B, I show Scriptural evidence (Genesis 1:5, 1:14-15) that God's intention was to define time in terms of the *earth's* rotation and the *earth's* motion around the sun, thus speaking of periods of time in our own frame of reference. This is quite reasonable in a book intended to be understood by people of widely different cultures and degrees of scientific knowledge. Therefore, it looks as if the Bible is telling us that God made the universe in six days E.S.T.—Earth Standard Time.

Chapter 2

Creation Week: A Possible Scenario

Some Major Events in Creation Week Considered

Although the problem of the starlight travel time has been solved in principle, it is important to try to apply these insights to the actual events of Creation Week. What follows is how I imagine these events to have taken place. Please keep in mind that the details of what follows are tentative and subject to drastic revision as we learn more. (For example, instead of the scenario below, God may have simply started with a white hole.) The validity of the basic White-Hole cosmology (answering as it does the objections, based on starlight, to recent creation) does not depend on all the following details being exactly as I have envisaged them.

For the reasoning behind these details, see Appendices B and C. I will concentrate on how God *may* have used some of the physical laws He Himself invented, but please keep in mind that He could and did supersede physical law at many points along the way. (The Bible verses following in italics in this chapter are my own translation.)

Day One (Genesis 1:1-5)

In the beginning God created the heavens and the earth. And the earth was formless and void, and darkness was on the face of the deep. And the spirit of God was moving on the face of the waters.

God creates a large 3-D space and within it a ball of liquid water, the "deep." The ball is greater than two light-years in diameter, large enough to contain all the mass of the universe (Appendix C). Two light-years is surprisingly small compared to the later size of the universe, but it is still huge (about 12 trillion miles or 20 trillion kilometers) compared to us, being more than a thousand times greater than the diameter of our solar system. Imagine floating on the face of the deep and gazing down into its unimaginable depths! That is why I think God called it "the deep."

Because of the great concentration of matter, this ball of water is deep within a black hole, whose event horizon is more than half a billion light-years away. The earth at this point is merely a formless, undefined region of water at the center of the deep, empty of inhabitant or feature. The deep is rotating slowly and there is no visible light at its

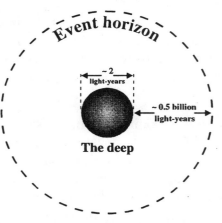

Figure 6 The Deep and the Event Horizon (*not* to scale)

surface. Figure 6 shows the deep at the instant God creates it. The spherical event horizon is not shown to scale, since it is very far away.

Because the enormous mass of the whole universe is contained in a ball of (relatively) small size, the gravitational force on the deep is very strong, more than a million trillion "g"s. This force compresses the deep very rapidly toward the center, making it extremely hot and dense. The heat rips apart the water molecules, atoms, even the nuclei into elementary particles.

And God said, "Let there be light"; and there was light.

Thermonuclear fusion reactions begin, forming heavier nuclei from lighter ones and liberating huge amounts of energy. As a consequence, an intense light illuminates the interior, breaking through to the surface and ending the darkness there.

And God saw that the light was good; and God separated the light from the darkness.

This paragraph following is the most speculative of my reconstruction of events. As the compression continues, gravity becomes so strong that light can no longer reach the surface, re-darkening it. Psalm 104:2, "Covering Thyself with light as with a cloak," in context appears to refer to Day One. This suggests to me that at this point the Spirit of God, "moving [or 'hovering'] over the surface of the waters" (Genesis 1:2), becomes a light source, in the same way as He will again become a light source at a future time (Revelation 21:23, 22:5). This would give the deep a bright side and a dark side, thus dividing light from darkness and inscribing "a circle on the face of the waters, at the boundary of light and darkness" (Job 26:10).

And God called the light day, and the darkness He called night. And there was evening and there was morning, one day.

The deep speeds up its rotation as the compression continues, as a whirling ice skater speeds up when she brings her arms inward. We can imagine a reference point on the surface rotating around to the dark side and continuing further around to the bright side again, marking off evening and morning. Rough calculations show that all of the events from the beginning to this point had to take place in a very short time, much less than a year. To calculate the time exactly would go beyond the frontiers of modern relativity, but I suspect that a modern clock (if it could survive) on the surface of the deep would register about 24 hours from the instant of Creation to the end of Day One.

Day Two (Genesis 1:6-8)

And God said, "Let there be an expanse in the midst of the waters, and let it separate the waters from the waters." And God made the expanse, and separated the waters which were below the expanse from the waters which were above the expanse.

By direct intervention (see Appendix C for more detail) God begins stretching out space, causing the ball of matter to expand rapidly, thus changing the black hole to a white hole. He marks off a large volume, the "expanse" ("firmament" in the KJV) within the deep, wherein material is allowed to pull apart into fragments and clusters as it expands, but He requires the "waters below" and the "waters above" the expanse to stay coherently together (Figure 7).

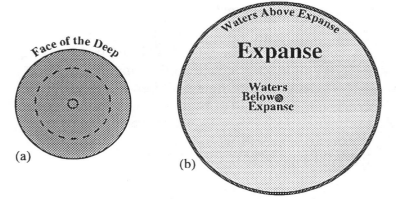

Figure 7 (a) Waters just before expansion.
(b) At instant of twofold expansion.

Normal physical processes cause cooling to proceed as rapidly as the expansion. Heat waves are stretched out to much longer wavelengths as a relativistic consequence of the stretching of space. Eventually these stretched-out waves will become the cosmic microwave background radiation (Appendix C).

Matter beneath the expanse expands until the surface reaches ordinary or present temperatures, becoming liquid water underneath an atmosphere. God collects various heavier atoms beneath the surface (formed from fusion reactions as mentioned earlier) and constructs minerals of them, laying "the foundations of the earth" (Job 38:4), i.e., its core and mantle. Gravity at the surface drops to normal or present values. Out in the expanse, matter is drawn apart, leaving irregular clusters of hydrogen, helium, and other atoms formed by the nuclear processes of the first day. The waters above the expanse stay together.

And God called the expanse "heavens." And there was evening and there was morning, a second day.

These heavens are interstellar space. Since the sun has not yet been created, the Spirit of God continues to be the light source close to the rotating waters below, giving them a light and dark side. The expansion started at the beginning of this day will continue until at least the end of the fourth day.

Day Three (Genesis 1:9-13)

And God said, "Let the waters under the heavens be gathered into one place, and let the dry land appear," and it was so.

Rapid radioactive decay occurs (see chapter on this subject in the forthcoming book), possibly as a consequence of the rapid stretching of space. The resulting heating forms the earth's crust and makes it buoyant relative to the mantle rock below it, causing the crust to rise above the waters, thus gathering the waters into ocean basins. I hypothesize that rapid volume cooling of molten rock deep within the earth also occurs, again as a result of the rapid expansion of space (Appendix C), solidifying the rock.

And God said, "Let the earth sprout vegetation. . ."

God makes plants on the newly formed land.

The continuing expansion of space causes the waters above the heavens to reach the event horizon and pass beyond it. This causes the amount of matter within the event horizon to begin decreasing, which in turn causes the event horizon to begin rapidly shrinking (remember the fat man on a strict diet) toward the earth. There are no stars yet, only clusters of hydrogen, helium, and other atoms left behind in the expanse by the rapid expansion.

The Day the Universe Opened (Genesis 1:14-19)

And God said, "Let there be lights in the expanse of the heavens . . . to give light on the earth," and it was so.

The shrinking event horizon reaches earth early on the morning of the fourth day. During this ordinary day as measured on earth, billions of years worth of physical processes take place in the distant cosmos. In particular, gravity has time to make distant clusters of hydrogen and helium atoms more compact.

And God made the two great lights . . . the stars also. And God gave them in the expanse of the heavens to give light on the earth. . . .

Early on the fourth morning, God coalesces the clusters of atoms into stars and thermonuclear fusion ignites in them. The newly-formed stars find themselves grouped together in galaxies and clusters of galaxies. As the fourth day proceeds on earth, the more distant stars age billions of years, while their light also has the same billions of years to travel to the earth. While the light is on its way, space continues to expand, relativistically stretching out the light waves (Appendix C) and shifting the wavelengths toward the red side of the spectrum. Stars which are now farthest away have the greatest redshift, because the waves have been stretched the most. This progressive redshift is exactly what is observed.

The Completed Universe (Genesis 1:31)

And God saw all that He had made, and behold, it was very good. And there was evening and there was morning, the sixth day.

God stops the expansion (see Appendix B) before the evening of the sixth day. Therefore, Adam and Eve, gazing up for the first time into the new night sky, can now see the Milky Way, the Andromeda galaxy, and all the other splendors in the heavens that declare the glory of God.

The author's book *Thousands, not Billions* will have exciting, easy-to-understand evidences for a young earth and universe, as well as a chapter that will essentially be the substance of this book. Also a section on the issue of radiometric dating. Anticipated release time is early 1996.

Readers prior to that date may place early orders/expressions of interest in this book by writing to the publisher or one of the following addresses:

United States:

> Master Books
> P.O. Box 26060
> Colorado Springs, CO 80936, U.S.A.
> Toll-free phone: 1-800-999-3777

Australia:

> Creation Science Foundation Ltd.
> P.O. Box 6302
> Acacia Ridge D.C. QLD 4110, Australia
> Phone: (07)273-7650

United Kingdom and Europe:

> Creation Science Foundation (U.K.)
> P. O. Box 1427
> Sevenhampton, Swindon
> Wilts., SN6 7UF, England
> Phone: (01793)512-268

New Zealand:

> Creation Science Foundation (N.Z.)
> Fowey Lodge, 215 Bleakhouse Road
> Howick, Auckland, New Zealand
> Phone: (09)534-8914

Contents of Appendices

Appendix A
Notes on Previous Related
Creationist Theories

Appendix B
A Biblical Basis for
Creationist Cosmology

Appendix C
Progress Toward a Young-Earth
Relativistic Cosmology

Appendices B and C are reprints of two technical
papers delivered at the Third International Conference
on Creationism, July 18–23, 1994, Pittsburgh.

Address:

Creation Science Fellowship, Inc.
362 Ashland Ave.
Pittsburgh, PA 15228, U.S.A.

Appendix A

Notes on Previous Related Creationist Theories

1. Mature Creation

A large number of creationists has favored this theory for many decades (see the astrophysics paper in Appendix C for references). I myself held it as a young creationist. Also called the "created-in-transit" theory, it holds that when God created all the particles in the universe, He also instantaneously created, in transit along their paths, all the light waves which would have been emitted by those particles for billions of years prior to their creation. Thus, He would have created a cosmos filled with light waves, all traveling in various directions toward various destinations.

It is certainly possible that God could have done such a thing, but I now know of five problems with the idea:

(1) Its proponents cite *no decisive Biblical support* for it, i.e., statements in the Bible which would clearly favor this theory over another. Furthermore, it appears that there is *no Biblical reason* for God to have set up such an illusion. For example, the seeming age of Adam is made necessary by God's desire to create him as a mature adult. But in contrast, proponents of the

theory offer no particular reason why God could not have done away with the necessity for illusion by simply letting us see only as much of the universe as a simple interpretation of the speed of light would permit. Except for parts of the Milky Way, most of the stars visible to the naked eye are closer than 6000 light-years.

(2) *Most of the events astronomers observe would never have happened.* For example consider a star explosion which astronomers observed in early 1987. This bright explosion, called Supernova 1987a, took place in one of the Magellanic Clouds (see introduction), about 160,000 light-years away from us. It was visible to the naked eye, and astronomers were (and are) very excited about it.

According to the "in-transit" theory, during creation week God would have made, about 6000 light-years away from us along the path between us and the Magellanic clouds, the light-wave images of an exploding star. He would also have had to have made the high-energy particles (gamma rays and neutrinos), as observed, from the exploded supernova. At the same instant of creation, further out along the path, He would have made images of an already-exploded star and its expanding shell of debris.

To be consistent, at the end of the 160,000 light-year path, God would also during creation week have made an actual supernova remnant (a "dead" neutron star), seemingly 160,000 years old, with a large debris shell around it.

But according to the "in-transit" theory, in spite of the images and particles astronomers observed, no actual supernova explosion would have ever happened!

This sort of fictional interpretation of events that we see in the sky would deny astronomy most of its value as a study of the real world. It would make the study of distant stars into a kind of theological literary criticism—a study of the fiction God would have chosen to write for us in the sky. And if most of what the heavens declare to us were fictional, then according to Psalm 19:1 ("The heavens declare the glory of God"), most of the glory of God would also be fictional. This philosophical-theological problem does not bother some supporters of the "in-transit" theory, but it disturbs many other people, including myself.

(3) The theory has *little explanatory power*. For example, it explains neither galactic red shifts nor the cosmic microwave background, except to say that for some incomprehensible reason God chose to support the Big Bang theory by manufacturing seeming evidence for it in the sky.

(4) The theory is *untestable,* because it makes no scientific predictions.

(5) The theory *discourages deeper investigation.* It reminds me of the 17th-century theory that the fossils were created by God just to puzzle men and test their faith! If all creationists had remained content with such a view of the fossils,

we would today be denied the tremendous explanatory power of flood geology. In a similar way, we should not remain content with the "created-in-transit" theory, lest we overlook a much better explanation.

2. Moon-Spencer Theory

From the 1960's through the early 1980's, some creationists promoted a paper published by Parry Moon and Domina Spencer in the August, 1953 issue of the *Journal of the Optical Society of America*. Moon and Spencer proposed that light somehow takes a shortcut in its path to us (through "Riemannian space"), traveling no more than 15 light-years to reach us even from the most distant galaxies.

I have always had a problem with that paper. All of our distance measurements are based on the characteristics of the light we see (parallax, angular size, light intensity, etc.). If the light were traveling only short distances, why would it have the characteristics of having traveled much greater distances? References 2 and 7 of the astrophysics paper in Appendix C point out other severe problems with the Moon-Spencer theory. The theory was never very popular, perhaps because of its obscurity, and it seems to have died of natural causes.

3. Decay in the Speed of Light

In 1979, Paul Steidl briefly proposed that the speed of light, c, might have been much greater in the past (ref. 47 of Appendix C, pp. 223–224). In the 1980's,

Barry Setterfield propounded the same idea much more vigorously, culminating in a widely distributed monograph on the topic in 1986 (ref. 35 of Appendix C). He cited a 20th-century analysis of 17th-century astronomical data indicating that the speed of light 300 years ago was about 2.6% higher than today's value. Setterfield also offered statistical analyses of about 160 other historical measurements showing that the speed of light had decayed smoothly from the 17th-century value, leveling off at today's value in about the year 1960. Fitting a curve to the data, he extrapolated the curve back into time, getting a value for the speed of light about 6000 years ago which was millions of times greater than today's value. He explored some of the theoretical consequences of such a decay in c, for example proposing it as an explanation for galactic red shifts (which later turned out to be in error).

Setterfield's c-decay theory generated tremendous initial enthusiasm among creationists—including myself. But as we examined the theory more carefully, some of us—including myself—began to find serious flaws. A vigorous scientific debate followed. The sharpest division of the debate centered on which statistical methods should be used. Critics of c-decay said that all 160 historical measurements should be lumped together into one analysis to avoid being misled by "tracking," which is the alleged "tendency of researchers to report an experimental result close to the results of their predecessors." Supporters of c-decay denied that tracking can occur. They preferred to break the 160 measurements into smaller groups (according to the experimental method used) and analyze each group separately. The critics tended to have more personal experience in experimental observations; the supporters tended to be more mathematical, doing more sophisticated statistical analyses. The intensity of the statistical part of the debate suggested to me that the data were in the shadowy borderland between randomness and reality, giving not enough support to either side to allow a clear victory.

However, I think both sides would agree that Setterfield's results are very strongly influenced by the 17th- and early 18th-century astronomical data, and that without those points on the graph, the seeming decay trend would be much weaker, perhaps non-existent. At the 1990 meeting of the International Conference on Creationism, physicist Eugene Chaffin outlined a careful re-analysis he was doing of those data. As a check on his analysis, Chaffin made his own set of astronomical observations, using the same methods as the 17th-century astronomers, but with more accurate instruments. As of 1990 his results were indeterminate, and he said so, causing both sides to acknowledge that Chaffin was neutral in the debate.

Late in 1992, Chaffin (ref. 8 of Appendix C) published his final result: the speed of light in the 17th century was within 0.4% of today's value. That value is within the experimental error of the early instruments used, and it is considerably below the 2.6% value Setterfield used. Chaffin also pointed out a clear example of "tracking" cited by Richard Feynmann in another area of experimental physics. Chaffin's work has dealt a serious blow to the *c*-decay theory, and many of its former supporters have now given up on it. As I point out in the acknowledgments for Appendix C, Setterfield's theory prompted me to work on the one I am presenting in this book.

4. Heating of Galactic Gas and Dust

The creationist theories above try to deal with light transit time (and number 3 tried to deal with galactic red shifts). However, they do not address the cosmic microwave background (CMB) radiation (see Appendix C for a description of this phenomenon). The only creationist model I know of for the CMB is one proposed in 1981 by Russell Akridge, Thomas Barnes, and Harold Slusher (ref. 1 of Appendix C). They showed that starlight could heat gas and dust in many parts of our galaxy to a temperature of several Kelvin (degrees above absolute zero) in just thousands of years.

Then they made an unfortunate assumption: *"Since there is only one measured blackbody spectrum as far as we know* [italics added], *and since galactic gas and dust heating does occur, the one spectrum must be due to galactic dust and gas."* The fact is that in certain directions, particularly directions in the plane of our galaxy, there are indeed other spectra, thus negating the assumption. Some of these warmer sources (typically a few dozen Kelvin) are indeed probably due to starlight heating of gas and dust. In the recent studies by the Cosmic Blackbody Explorer (COBE) satellite team, such known sources were subtracted out. Some of the most publicized pictures of the COBE results show these sources before subtraction as a bright irregular band along the galactic plane.

The best evidence for the CMB comes from directions perpendicular to the plane of our galaxy, where we are often able to see clearly, without hindrance of dust or gas, light in the visible spectrum from galaxies billions of light-years away. From those directions we also see the CMB radiation coming in with remarkable uniformity. The mean free path of a microwave photon under such circumstances is not hugely different from that of a visible light photon, so the source of the CMB must be at least billions of light-years away. This excludes the Akridge-Barnes-Slusher (ABS) model, which took no account of mean free paths or opacities.

Even if one insisted that the CMB sources are only within our galaxy, it is very difficult to imagine why dust in different parts of the galaxy should all be within one part in 100,000 of the same temperature everywhere, considering that the illumination by starlight (which is supposed to be heating the dust) varies by many orders of magnitude from place to place in the galaxy.

I should also caution the reader that the ABS paper had some serious misunderstandings about Big Bang cosmology: (1) the paper did not acknowledge the unbounded nature of those theories, and (2) it showed no understanding of how the expansion of space itself would, according to general relativity, cause red shifts in the wavelengths of CMB photons, without any interaction with matter being required.

Summary

It is commendable that all four of these models were trying to grapple with the cosmological data. But none of them deals with all three of the large-scale cosmic phenomena I cite in Appendix C. Furthermore, none of their proponents cite decisive Biblical support, that is, clear Scriptures which would favor one theory over another. Theory 1 cannot be disproved scientifically (since it makes no testable predictions), but it has disturbing theological and philosophical implications. I would regard it as a theory of last resort, to be used only after many, more ambitious theories have been carefully investigated and rejected. Theories 2 through 4 appear to me and many other creationist scientists to have been falsified by the data, though a few remaining supporters of each theory might disagree. Clearly, none of these theories has emerged with a consensus of support from creationist scientists. We need more and better creationist cosmologies. I say "more" because mine may prove to have fatal flaws of its own, but if we have a *variety* of good theories to choose from, we are much more likely to find the truth.

Appendix B

A BIBLICAL BASIS FOR CREATIONIST COSMOLOGY

D. RUSSELL HUMPHREYS, Ph.D.
Creation Science Fellowship of New Mexico
P.O. Box 10550, Albuquerque, NM 87184

ABSTRACT
Taking Genesis 1 and other scriptures in the most straightforward possible sense leads to several conclusions of great importance for cosmology: (1) The "expanse" of Genesis chapter 1 is not the earth's atmosphere but interstellar space, (2) The "waters above the expanse" are cosmic in scale and represent a boundary for interstellar space, (3) the earth is near the center of the universe. These conclusions form the basis for a young-earth relativistic cosmology which I describe in another paper (Appendix C) presented at this conference.

KEYWORDS
Biblical cosmology, young-earth creationism, age of universe, hermeneutics.

1. INTRODUCTION

> *To him that rideth upon the heavens of heavens,*
> *which were of old* — Psalm 68:33, KJV.

The Bible lays a good foundation for a young-earth relativistic cosmology. That is the main point I want to make in this paper. Contrary to impressions made by the news media, no one today can start from observed data and build up a cosmology by rigorous scientific deduction. Instead, some ideological initial assumptions are necessary, as cosmologists Stephen Hawking and George Ellis [5, p. 134] acknowledge:

> ... we are not able to make cosmological models
> without some admixture of ideology.

53

All the major cosmologies of this century, including the "big-bang" cosmologies, start with an arbitrary assumption which Hawking and Ellis call the *Copernican principle* [5, p.134]. Reduced to its essence, the Copernican principle requires matter in the universe to be *unbounded*, that is, the distribution of stars and galaxies in the cosmos can have no edges and no center. When cosmologists plug this assumption into the equations of Einstein's general theory of relativity and turn the mathematical crank, the Big Bang and other famous cosmologies follow logically as a result.

In this paper I list evidence that the most straightforward understanding of the relevant scriptures gives us a cosmos which contradicts the Copernican principle. That is, the distribution of stars and galaxies in the biblical cosmos has a clearly-defined edge and a center. Moreover the earth would be, on a cosmological scale of distances, near the center. In another paper at this conference (Appendix C), I show that putting this condition of boundedness into the equations of general relativity results in a cosmos which is radically different than the conventional cosmologies. In this new picture of the cosmos, gravity and black hole physics play a central role.

In particular, an experimentally-measured general relativistic effect, called *gravitational time dilation* by some authors [10, p. 21], causes clocks (and all physical processes) to tick at different rates in different parts of the universe. (This is not the more familiar "velocity" time dilation of special relativity.) By this effect on time itself, God could have made the universe in six ordinary days as measured on earth, while still allowing time for light to travel billions of light-years to reach us by natural means. The theory also appears to explain the two other major cosmological phenomena we see: the red shifts of light from distant galaxies and the cosmic microwave background radiation. Thus, this biblical foundation appears to lead to a young-earth cosmology which is consistent with Einstein's general theory of relativity and astronomical observations. As measured by clocks on earth, the age of the universe today could be as small as the face-value biblical age of about 6000 years.

Before we examine the relevant scriptures, I want to clarify my approach to them in the next section.

2. UNDERSTANDING SCRIPTURE STRAIGHTFORWARDLY

A basic premise of modern creationism is that the Bible is an accurate message from God to man, including matters of science, and intended to be understood and used, as set forth in 2 Timothy 3:16,17:

> All Scripture is inspired by God and profitable for teaching, for reproof, for correction, for training in righteousness; that the man of God may be adequate, equipped for every good work.

(All quotes in English are from the *New American Standard Bible*, unless otherwise indicated.) To be useful in this way, the message must be understandable, and that raises the question of how to "interpret" scripture. Scripture itself provides some guidance on that point. For example, consider Proverbs 8:8,9, where wisdom, personified as a woman, says:

> All the utterances of my mouth are in righteousness;
> There is nothing crooked or perverted in them.
> They are all *straightforward* to him who understands,
> And right to those who find knowledge.

The word "straightforward" (KJV "plain") here is from the Hebrew word נכח(*nakoach*), which one lexicon [6, p. 238] translates as "lying straight ahead ... straight, right." So the words of a wise person are characteristically straightforward. They are not "crooked or perverted," that is, they are not intended to deceive the hearer. According to Proverbs 8:22, Jehovah possesses this wisdom, and so we would expect His words to be straightforward. There may be great depth to His words, but *any deeper understandings should be encompassed within the plain, face-value meaning* of the words as they would be understood by a speaker of Hebrew or Greek in the time and place where they were first given to men. Anything else would lead to deception, which the passage says is not characteristic of wisdom.

A caution is necessary at this point. While recognizing that God is the ultimate author of the Bible, some theologians nonetheless insist that we should not look for any more meaning in scripture than its *human* intermediaries intended:

> In other words, in answer to the question, "How much scientific truth can one extract from Genesis 1?" the answer must be: "One can extract only that which the writer himself, Moses, intended to teach." [3, p. 13]

The motive of this theologian was good; he wanted to guard against the natural tendency of people to read into scripture meanings not included within the bounds of the normal meanings of the words. But good motives do not always produce good principles, and here I think the principle is clearly wrong. First of all, it is not scriptural. For example, the same Peter who wrote about the inspiration of scripture, " ... men moved by the Holy Spirit spoke from God" (2 Peter 1:21), also wrote that inspired prophets did not immediately understand fully what the Holy Spirit was moving them to say:

> As to this salvation, the prophets who prophesied of the grace that would come to you made careful search and inquiry, seeking to know what person or time the Spirit of Christ within them was indicating as He predicted the sufferings of Christ and the glories to follow — *1 Peter 1:10,11.*

If these prophets had fully understood what they were saying as they were saying it, they would not after that have had to make "careful search and inquiry, seeking to know ..." If we were to limit ourselves to the intent of the speaker or writer as he spoke or wrote, this passage says we would miss a lot of rich truth. Secondly, the principle essentially shuts us away from God and what He intended to say to us. We don't study Genesis in order to know the mind of Moses; we study to know the mind of *God.*

A straightforward approach to scripture is the only one I can think of which can yield surprising new knowledge. Without such an approach, I would tend to re-interpret any passage of scripture which did not fit into what I thought was true at the time, and scripture would lose its power to astonish me. If God intended scripture to inform us of things we would not otherwise know, then He must also have intended it to be understood straightforwardly. "Straightforward" does not necessarily always mean "literal." Someone who reads straightforwardly recognizes the metaphors in scripture, while someone who reads literally will try to squeeze a metaphor into a concrete straitjacket. But when we come to a possible metaphor, we ought to try on some literal meanings for size. If we find one that seems to fit, we ought to go with that meaning as a working hypothesis until we find good reason in scripture to think otherwise.

To make these points a little clearer, imagine a young Jewish Christian of the first century who understands Greek, Hebrew, and the scriptures well. Let's call him "Timothy," since Paul's protege was like that. But let's also imagine that this Timothy knows nothing of the advanced scientific knowledge of his day, such as Aristotle's works. All that Timothy knows is from either everyday experience or careful study of scripture, which Paul says is sufficient to give us wisdom (2 Tim. 3:15). Now if scripture really is straightforward and sufficient, then the meaning Timothy derives from the words is probably the meaning that God intended everybody to get. For example, when Timothy reads in Exodus 20:11,

> For in six days the LORD made the heavens and the earth, the sea and all that is in them, and rested on the seventh day; therefore the LORD blessed the sabbath day and made it holy,

he notices that the context is that of ordinary days of the week. Not having *Scientific American* to tell him that the earth is billions of years old, Timothy is not looking for loopholes in this statement. Instead he simply concludes that scripture is saying Jehovah made the whole universe in six ordinary weekdays. My point is that if scripture is what it claims to be, then we ought to take Timothy's view of the passage and not try to twist the words into new meanings compatible with *Scientific American*'s worldview, or for that matter into anyone else's worldview.

Of all people, young-earth creationists probably take scripture the most straightforwardly. For example, see Robert Walsh's article on hermeneutics [14]. But I find that even we are prone to abandon that principle when it runs counter to some teaching or model we cherish. In this paper I intend, when presented with two or more interpretations of a passage, to apply the "Timothy test" and choose the most straightforward.

3. THE EXPANSE IS INTERSTELLAR SPACE

> *And God made the expanse, and separated the*
> *waters which were below the expanse from the*
> *waters which were above the expanse; and it was*
> *so. And God called the expanse heavens* —
> Genesis 1:7,8, my translation.

One question that leaps to mind when we first encounter the verses above is: What is the "expanse" (KJV "firmament")? The King James version's word appears to come from the Vulgate's word *firmamentum*, which in turn appears to stem from the Septuagint's translation, στερέωμα (*stereoma*). These three translations emphasize 3-dimensional solidity (*stereo-*) and firmness, about which I will say more in section 7. The Hebrew word is רקיע (*raqia*), meaning "extended surface" [1, p. 956]. Lexicons [2, p. 591] say it comes from the verb רקע (*raqa*), whose primary meaning is "to stamp ... stamp down ... spread out" [6, p. 347]. One 19th-century lexicon [2, p. 692], uncontaminated by 20th-century cosmology, adds to the list of the verb's meanings the interesting phrase "to expand." I will say more about that meaning in section 7. But aside from what learned commentators think, Genesis 1:14-17 gives some direct information about the expanse, which God also called "heavens":

> Then God said, let there be lights *in* the expanse
> of the heavens ... and let them be for lights *in* the
> expanse of the heavens ... and God made the two
> great lights ... He made the stars also. And God
> placed them *in* the expanse of the heavens to give
> light on the earth.

In this passage I have italicized the little word "in" to emphasize an important point: the sun, moon, and stars are *in* the expanse. The Hebrew for "in" here is the prefix ב (*b*ᵉ), which has essentially the same range of meanings as the English word "in" [6, p. 32].

Now imagine what the Timothy of Section 2 would think about the expanse from this passage. I think everyone would agree that he would simply say the expanse is the place where the sun, moon, and stars are. Therefore, the "Timothy test" leads me to conclude that the most straightforward understanding of this passage is that *the expanse is interstellar space.* Using our knowledge of the distances of heavenly bodies, that means that the waters above the expanse must now be at cosmic distances from us, billions of light-years away!

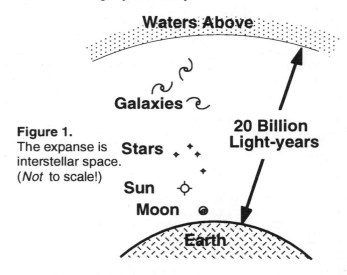

Figure 1.
The expanse is interstellar space.
(*Not* to scale!)

4. THE EXPANSE IS NOT MERELY THE ATMOSPHERE

As most creationists will recognize, the above reading of scripture conflicts with the venerable "vapor canopy" model, which holds that the expanse is merely the earth's atmosphere and that the "waters above" were a canopy of water vapor immediately above the atmosphere [3]. (Canopy theorists correctly argue that the "waters above" had to have been a large amount of water distinctly above the expanse and could not have been mere clouds in the atmosphere [3, pp. 48-58].) The canopy is supposed to have been related to the "windows of the heavens" of Genesis 7:11, and the canopy, by collapsing during the Genesis flood, is supposed to have provided some of the waters of the flood.

Advocates of the canopy model seem to have assumed without much consideration that the expanse is only the earth's atmosphere [3, p. 47]. However, two of them [15. p. 229] use an English translation of Genesis 1:20 as support for that idea:

> ... and let birds fly above the earth in the open expanse of the heavens.

The phrase "in the open expanse," used in most English translations, implies that the expanse is what birds fly in. In my early years as a creationist, I thought that was a sufficient justification for the canopy model. However, one day I discovered that the actual Hebrew phraseology is quite different. In the following paragraph I have reproduced the last part of Genesis 1:20 from an interlinear Hebrew Bible [4, p. 1]. Read it from right to left:

וְעוֹף֙ יְעוֹפֵ֣ף עַל־הָאָ֔רֶץ עַל־פְּנֵ֖י רְקִ֥יעַ הַשָּׁמָֽיִם׃

and	let fly	over	the	on	the	the	the
birds	around		earth		face	expanse	heavens
					of	of	

So the literal Hebrew doesn't have "in the open expanse." It doesn't even have the preposition "in." Instead it uses another preposition, עַל ('al), which means "on, over, above," but not "in" [6, p. 272]. Moreover, the word here translated "open" comes from the word פנה (paneh), whose primary meaning is "face" [6, p. 293]. I can't find "open" listed as a secondary meaning for paneh in any of my lexicons [6, p. 293] [1, p. 815] [2, p. 627]. The passage literally says "on the face of the expanse of the heavens." It is the same phraseology as in Genesis 1:2, which is correctly translated, "on the face of" the deep. In biblical usage, the "face"

Figure 2.
The atmosphere is only the *face* of the expanse.

The Rest of the Expanse

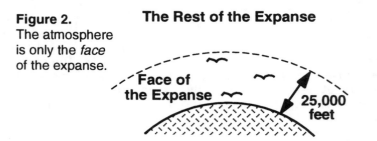

can be oriented in any direction, and what is "on" it need not be gravitationally above it (e.g., Exodus 34:33 and Genesis 11:28, Hebrew). Looking up into the sky, we see birds flying across it, and the passage says what they are flying in is merely at the surface of the expanse. Birds can fly up to altitudes of 25,000 feet [9, p. 785], at which point they are above two-thirds of the atoms of the atmosphere. So most of the atmosphere is merely at the surface of the expanse. Therefore the expanse itself must be something much bigger — such as interstellar space.

Thus, the only verse allegedly justifying the identification of the atmosphere with the whole expanse really supports the idea of the expanse being interstellar space!

I also have a "prepositional" problem with the canopy model: If the expanse were really only the atmosphere, then a better preposition to use in verses 14,15, and 17 would have been 'al, which as I mentioned means "on" or "above." Then the verses would tell us that sun, moon, and stars were "*above* the expanse of the heavens." But the verses don't use that preposition.

Some people say that God let the stars "appear" as if they were in the atmosphere, even though they were really above it. One problem with that view is that God did not use the word "appear" in connection with the expanse, even though in Genesis 1:9 He did use it in connection with the appearing of the dry land. However, the main problem is with the straightforwardness principle. If even you or I can think of simple ways to say the stars are above the expanse or only appeared to be in it, then why wouldn't God do so in the interest of accuracy? Perhaps He refrained from saying so because it would be inaccurate for Him to imply the expanse is merely the atmosphere.

Another biblical problem with the canopy model is Psalm 148:1-4, which mentions the "waters above":

Praise the LORD!	Praise Him, all His hosts!
Praise the LORD from the heavens;	Praise Him, sun and moon;
Praise Him in the heights!	Praise Him, all stars of light!
Praise Him, all His angels;	Praise Him, highest heavens,
	And the *waters that are above the heavens*!

First notice the context in which these waters appear: "heavens ... heights ... sun and moon ... stars ... highest heavens." This suggests that the waters belong 'way out there with all those other heavenly objects, not close to the earth. Next, notice the timing. The canopy model says the waters above the expanse of the heavens collapsed at the Genesis flood, but this Psalm, written after the flood, implies the waters above the heavens still exist in the present. In fact, verses 5 and 6 of the same Psalm say that the waters and the heavens are to last at least as long as the time of this physical universe endures:

> Let them praise the name of the LORD,
> For he commanded and they were created.
> He has also established them forever and ever;
> He has made a decree which will not pass away.

But if the waters are to endure "forever and ever" above the heavens, then they can't have collapsed.

A last biblical problem is with how the waters of the Genesis flood ceased:

> Also the fountains of the deep and the floodgates
> of the sky were closed, and the rain from the sky
> was restrained — *Genesis 8:2.*

Notice the account doesn't say the waters from above stopped themselves because there were none left to collapse. Instead it implies there were still some waters available, and that they had to be stopped by closing the floodgates of the sky (literally "the windows of the heavens"). In line with this, Malachi 3:10 implies that the "windows of the heavens," whatever they are, still exist. These verses do not fit very well with the concept of a collapsing vapor canopy. Thus the canopy model has considerable biblical problems. To me the most serious one is simply that the most straightforward interpretation excludes it.

5. A CANOPY IS NOT SCIENTIFICALLY NECESSARY
As a younger creationist, I found that one of the great attractions of the canopy model for me was that its logical consequences would provide an explanation of several scientific problems for creationists. The most important of these consequences were: (1) a "greenhouse" effect to make the warm, uniform pre-flood climate indicated by the fossils; and (2) a shielding of cosmic rays to reduce carbon 14 in the pre-flood world, thus explaining "old" radiocarbon dates.

However, we now have very good scientific reasons [16] to think that the amount of carbon dioxide in the pre-flood atmosphere was many times greater than today. That would produce a strong greenhouse effect, a warm climate, and as a bonus, stimulate plant growth to produce the large amount of plant life we find in the fossils. The additional ordinary carbon in the biosphere would dilute carbon 14, so that the pre-flood $^{14}C/^{12}C$ ratio would be considerably lower due to that effect alone, thus explaining the "old" post-flood radiocarbon dates. In addition, we have evidence suggesting that the earth's magnetic field was at least ten times greater before the flood than now [7]. That would enable the geomagnetic field to be a very effective shield for cosmic rays, thus greatly reducing the production of carbon 14, making the pre-flood world a healthier place, and further explaining post-flood radiocarbon dates. Thus we have alternative scientific explanations for the main things the canopy model was supposed to explain.

For decades, creationist atmospheric scientists have put a lot of diligent work, some of it presented at these conferences, into scientifically modeling vapor canopies. I greatly respect their work, but it looks to me as if they still haven't got the problem solved. I also greatly respect the pioneers of modern scientific creationism, who in the first decades of their work developed the canopy model as part of the alternative worldview they were presenting.

However, the idea of a canopy atop the atmosphere did not come down from Sinai with Moses, engraved by the finger of God on the back side of the stone tablets. Instead, it was a human interpretation of scripture which was, for a time, the best understanding we could come up with. I think that time has passed. In spite of the large emotional investment some of us may have put into the canopy model, I suggest that now is a good time to re-evaluate the model, to see if it is worth any further effort. One thing to consider is whether other scriptures besides Genesis 1 can support the idea. If so, there need be no conflict between the cosmic-size expanse I am proposing and a vapor canopy over the pre-flood atmosphere. Lastly, if it is any comfort, my suggestion doesn't do away with a canopy of water; it simply raises it a bit higher — a cosmic canopy!

6. A BOUNDED UNIVERSE

The importance of the waters above the expanse is that they represent a boundary for the matter of the created universe. What is beyond that boundary? Take a look once more at the first two verses of Genesis:

> In the beginning God created the heavens and the earth. And the earth was formless and void, and darkness was over the surface of the deep; and the Spirit of God was moving over the surface of the waters.

The "deep" was the body of water within which God later, on day two, made the expanse, which He called "heavens" (Genesis 1:7,8). But notice that the deep has a *surface*. What is above that surface? I suggest that it is the "heavens" of Genesis 1:1. That is, on day one God made a space, called the heavens, which contained a large body of water, the deep. On day two he made the expanse, which He also called "heavens", within the waters. Thus there would be two heavens, the day-two heavens being a subset of the day-one heavens. This dual naming has a parallel in the case of the earth. Having created "the earth" as a formless body on day one (Genesis 1:1,2), God then on day three calls the dry land "earth" (Genesis 1:10). But the dry land (i.e., the continent or continents) is only a subset of the whole earth, which for example includes the seas also (Genesis 1:10). So there seem to be two meanings to the word "earth," one including the whole planet, the other limited to the dry land only. In the same way there would be two meanings to the word "heavens," the day-two heavens being the expanse, and the day-one heavens being the larger space in which the other created things exist.

Some theologians would object that Genesis 1:1 is a summary statement of all the work God would do later on in creation week, and so there would not be two heavens and two earths, but only one of each. Other theologians [11] argue strongly against that view, saying that the Hebrew phrasing favors consecutiveness from verse one to verse two. Another point is that if verse 1 is a summary of later work, then the account really begins with verse 2, leaving no statement at all about who created the matter of the earth and the deep. Thus we would no longer know for certain that God created the original matter; we would simply have an account of how He modified it. The theological consequences of that view would be major, and there would be severe inconsistences with the rest of scripture.

Thus the most straightforward view is that there are (at least) two spaces called "heavens." By this view, another scriptural name for the heavens of day one would be the "heavens of the heavens," שְׁמֵי הַשָּׁמַיִם (sh^{e}mai ha-shamaim), which is often translated "highest heavens," as in Psalm 148:4, NASB. Although this created heavens is larger, it also is of limited extent, since Solomon said it was not big enough to contain God:

> But will God indeed dwell on the earth? Behold, the heaven and heaven of heavens cannot contain thee; how much less this house that I have builded? — 1 Kings 8:27, KJV.

This verse alone should be enough to convince most creationists that the created universe is of finite extent. A finite cosmos could still be closed and unbounded; see Appendix C (section 5) for the distinctions. Above I said "at least" two heavens because Paul mentions a third heavens in 2 Corinthians 12:2 :

> I know a man in Christ who fourteen years ago — whether in the body I do not know, or out of the body I do not know, God knows — such a man was caught up to the third heaven.

Let's count up heavens. Numbering outward from earth, there is the *first* heavens, interstellar space, also known as the expanse, created on day two. The earth's atmosphere, by my view, is simply the face of the expanse. Above the first heavens, out beyond the most distant galaxy, is a wall of ordinary water (the surfaces of which are now probably ice), of unknown thickness. Beyond the outside surface of the waters is a space which I here call the *second* heavens, also called the heavens of heavens, the heavens of day one. We know very little about the second heavens, except that it is a created thing and is of finite extent. This space could be closed and unbounded, but the matter within it is bounded. Somewhere beyond the second heavens is the *third* heavens, about which we know little. Maybe that is where God lives. Anyhow, the simple answer to the question of what is beyond the waters above is: the second heavens.

7. THE EXPANSE HAS EXPANDED

A large number of Bible verses refer to God "stretching out" or "spreading out" the heavens. Here are some:

Who alone stretches out the heavens — *Job 9:8.*

Stretching out heaven like a tent curtain — *Psalm 104:2.*

Who stretches out the heavens like a curtain,
And spreads them out like a tent to dwell in — *Isaiah 40:22.*

He has stretched out the heavens — *Jeremiah 10:12.*

The LORD who stretches out the heavens—*Zechariah 12:1.*

There are at least 12 other similar verses in the Old Testament. Here is a list:

2 Sam. 22:10	Job 26:7	Job 37:18	Psalm 18:9
Psalm 144:5	Isaiah 42:5	Isaiah 44:24	Isaiah 45:12
Isaiah 48:13	Isaiah 51:13	Jer. 51:15	Ezekiel 1:22

In these verses the Hebrew words translated "stretch out" come from the verb נטה (*natah*), whose primary meaning is "extend, stretch out ... spread out" [6, p. 235]. In three of the verses (2 Samuel 22:10, Psalm 18:9, and Psalm 144:5) the verb is translated by a secondary meaning, "to bow." The Hebrew words translated "spread out" come from the verbs מתח (*matach*) "spread out", טפח (*taphach*) "spread out, extend", or רקע (*raqa*) "stamp, spread out." The last verb (from Job 37:18) is related to the noun "expanse" (*raqia*) mentioned in sect. 3.

So these 17 verses use four different verbs to communicate the idea of stretching and spreading. The verses occur in a wide variety of contexts throughout the Old Testament, generally as an illustration of God's great power. The frequency, diversity, and widespread locations of these verses led me to suspect in 1985 that they were more than mere metaphor.

If there is a more literal meaning, what is it? To answer that, we must consider more precisely what the heavens are, since they are the object of the stretching. First of all, the heavens cannot be the stars, because God made the heavens on days one and two, before He made the stars on day four. Moreover, many verses, such as Nehemiah 9:6, make a distinction between the heavens and "host" of the heavens, namely the things occupying the heavens. So the word "heavens" must be roughly equivalent to our word "space."

Generally we think of space as a vacuum, an empty volume. But how can a nothingness be stretched out as if it were a *something*, like a tent curtain? To get a clue, notice how scripture speaks of other things happening to the heavens. The heavens can be *torn* (Isaiah 64:1), *worn out* like a garment (Psalm 102:26), *shaken* (Hebrews 12:26, Haggai 2:6, Isaiah 13:13), *burnt up* (2 Peter 3:12), *split apart* like a scroll when it is rolled up (Revelation 6:14), and *rolled up* like a mantle (Hebrews 1:12) or a scroll (Isaiah 34:4). It certainly sounds like space itself is a material of some sort!

Interestingly enough, there are many phenomena in modern physics which point to such a concept (such as Maxwell's displacement current and vacuum polarization), and physics even offers an explanation of why we cannot perceive this medium through which we would be moving (Dirac's electron "sea" and Pauli's exclusion principle). The physics clues suggest that such a medium would be like an elastic solid. This might explain why the words *raqia, stereoma*, and *firmamentum* (see section 3) all seem to have some connection with solidity and firmness:

When He made firm the skies above — *Proverbs 8:28.*

Can you, with Him, spread out the skies,
Strong as a molten [cast] mirror? — *Job 37:18.*

Notice also the references to "rolling up" the heavens like a mantle or a scroll (Hebrews 1:12 and Isaiah 34:4). This suggests that (1) there is some dimension in which space is thin, (2) space can be bent, and (3) there exists a direction it can be bent toward. Thus these verses could be hinting that a fourth spatial dimension exists, even though we can't perceive it. (Time would be a fifth dimension, dealt with separately.) Again, this idea is not foreign to modern physics. See Appendix C (section 5) for the ramifications in general relativity.

So if space is a material, some kind of "stuff" and not a nothingness, then it can be stretched out like a tent curtain, etc. This corresponds exactly to the picture behind the general relativistic expansion of the cosmos, where it is space itself which is being stretched out. Again, see Appendix C (section 3) for the physics of this phenomenon.

In summary, the verses of this section imply that God stretched out space itself at some time in the past. Now let's consider when He did this. Certainly the second day of creation is a good candidate for the starting point, because that is when he made the "expanse." But was the stretching complete at the end of the second day? There is a clue which suggests the answer is "no." The second day is the only day in which God did not comment "good" about the things he had made that day. Yet on the sixth day, God saw that *all* things He had made were very good (Genesis 1:31). The "all" would include the expanse. I suggest that He didn't call it good on the second day because the expansion wasn't complete by that time. This reasoning would correspondingly imply that the expansion stopped on or before the sixth day. (The Hebrew of 2 Samuel 22:10 and Psalm 18:9 refers to stretching the heavens; the translations usually use a secondary meaning, namely "bow". If those passages refer to the Genesis flood, then it is possible that there was another episode of stretching during the flood. It is also possible that the expansion has been continuous from day two until now, although I consider that unlikely in the light of these verses and the above rationale.) Thus the heavens would have been complete by the time that Adam and Eve first saw them.

8. THE WATERS OF THE DEEP

> *And the earth was without form, and void; and darkness was upon the face of the deep. And the Spirit of God moved upon the face of the waters —*
> Genesis 1:2, KJV.

Ever since I first encountered this verse as a seven-year-old, I wondered what the "deep" in this verse was. The Hebrew word is תהום (*t^ehom*), which lexicons translate as "deep, sea, abyss ...

primaeval ocean ... depth" [1, p. 1062], "primeval ocean, deep ... deeps of sea ... subterranean water" [6, p. 386]. The Septuagint translates it as the ἄβυσσος, the abyss, "the immeasurable depth" [13, p. 2]. In this section let's consider the composition of the deep.

The first clue is the last word of the verse, "waters." That word caused the seven-year-old me to think that the deep was ordinary liquid water. As grownups, however, we might wonder if the Hebrew word used here for "waters" (מים, *mayim*) could include more sophisticated useages, such as "snow," "ice," "steam," "fluid," or even "plasma."

According to three Hebrew lexicons [6, p. 193] [1, p. 565] [2, p. 694], most occurrences of this word in the Old Testament refer literally to liquid water. A few other occurrences are as part of metaphors, such as "the hearts of the people melted and became as water" (Joshua 7:5), but even in those cases the metaphors would be meaningless if the word *mayim* did not refer to ordinary water. In the few remaining cases, there are other substances in the water, such as salt or poison, but they are still essentially water. If frozen or gaseous forms of water are meant, the Bible always uses other words, as far as I have been able to find. As for the physics concept of "plasma," the words for "fire" or "flame" would be more accurate, since fire is the most common thing in everyday human experience which contains some hot plasma. In summary, *all* of the approximately 580 other uses of the word in the Old Testament refer to ordinary liquid water. Thus, according to the Timothy test, the most straightforward interpretation of Genesis 1:2 is that the deep, or at least its surface, initially consisted of ordinary water at normal densities and temperatures.

9. THE DEPTH OF THE DEEP

> Then God said, "Let there be an expanse in the midst of the waters, and let it separate the waters from the waters." And God made the expanse, and separated the waters which were below the expanse from the waters which were above the expanse; and it was so — Genesis 1:6,7.

Now let's consider how big the deep was initially. Sections 3 and 4 show that the expanse is now of cosmic size, and Section 7 shows that it has expanded, so it must have started at a smaller size. In Appendix C (section 16) I surmise that God formed the stars from waters of the deep left behind by the expansion, so the mass of the visible universe would have been contained in the deep. A simple calculation in Appendix C (section 10) shows the mass is roughly 3×10^{51} kilograms. Lastly, I show evidence in the other paper that the universe is approximately spherical. So if the deep were similarly spherical (as it would be normally under the force of gravity), and if its waters were initially of ordinary density as Section 8 (pp. 68-69) affirms, then a simple calculation shows that its radius had to be at least *one light-year*. I say "at least" because we also need to account for the waters above the expanse, which are of undetermined thickness.

This is surprisingly small compared to the cosmos. However, it is still huge, about 10 trillion kilometers, more than a thousand times larger than the radius of our solar system. And yet it took years for the Voyager spaceprobes, travelling at very high speeds, to reach the edge of the solar system. Imagine floating on the face of the deep and gazing down into its immense depths! "The deep" is certainly an appropriate name. Further-more, a sphere of nothing but water is bottomless; if you plunged down to its center and kept going, you would start rising upward without ever having hit a solid bottom. So the Septuagint's word "the abyss" ("without bottom") is also a very appropriate name for the deep.

Notice that I said "how big the deep was *initially*." Strong gravitation was very likely in operation at the time of Genesis 1:2, in order to have a clearly-defined surface over a large body of liquid water in the presence of a vacuum (surface tension can't do it). The word "over" in Genesis 1:2 also hints at the existence of gravity by that time. If gravity was working normally, the gravitational force at the surface for the above mass and radius would be about 3×10^{17} (nearly a million trillion) times greater than at the earth's surface today. Appendix C (section 15) shows that if God let things proceed normally, these enormous gravitational forces would cause the deep to begin collapsing down toward the center.

Also, the huge gravitational forces would mean that the deep was far within a *black hole*. See Appendix C (section 11) for an outline of the physics of black holes. As I point out in that paper, one of the ramifications of being deep inside a black hole is that the collapse would take place very rapidly. As measured by either of the two types of clocks mentioned in my other paper, the collapse would take much less than a year, possibly a few days, to become an infinitely-small "singularity" at the center. However, the verses in the next section imply that God did not let the collapse proceed that far; you can't have a center in something infinitely small.

10. THE CENTER OF THE UNIVERSE

Since I've brought up the center of the deep several times, let's consider it more carefully. Notice the words "in the midst" in Genesis 1:6 :

> ... Let there be an expanse in the midst of the waters ...

The corresponding Hebrew word is בתוך (*b^{e}tok*), which is the preposition ב(*b^e*), "in," combined with the noun תוך (*tawek*) whose primary meaning is "midst, middle" [6, p. 387], "midst ... of a space or place," and with the preposition, "in the very heart and midst of" [1, p. 1063]. The middle of a sphere is its center, so the expanse must have started in the vicinity of the center. I say "in the vicinity" in order to leave some room for the approximate nature of the phrase.

Another clue is the word "below" in Genesis 1:7 :

> ... and separated the waters below the expanse
> from the waters which were above the expanse ...

The Hebrew translated word "below" is מתחת (*mittachath*), which consists of the preposition מן (*min*), "from," combined with the adjective תחת (*tachath*), meaning "under, beneath" [6, p. 389]. This word, along with "above," confirms that gravity was operating. It also suggests that the center of gravity was within the waters below, providing supporting evidence for the idea that the waters below were at or near the center.

Now let's consider in Genesis 1:9,10 what the "waters below the expanse" of the heavens became:

> Then God said, "Let the waters below the heavens be gathered into one place, and let the dry land appear"; and it was so. And God called the dry land earth, and the gathering of the waters he called seas; and God saw that it was good.

At this point, the waters below have become the continent(s) and seas of our own planet. Therefore during creation week, *the earth was at or near the center of the universe*. (I find nothing in the context to say that the earth was motionless with respect to the center, so it may have moved away from the center a bit since that time.)

11. TRANSFORMING THE WATERS

Section 8 has the original material of the creation being nothing but water. Yet Genesis 1:10 says that by day three dry land appeared, and dry land is obviously not water, but rather a collection of minerals containing silicon, iron, magnesium, calcium, carbon, oxygen, and many other elements. How did that happen? The apostle Peter gives us some additional insight on this point:

> ... by the word of God the heavens existed long ago and the earth was formed out of water and by water — *2 Peter 3:5.*

The word translated "formed" is the Greek participle συνεστῶσα (*sunestosa*), from the verb συνίστημι (*sunistemi*), whose primary meaning is "to place together, to set in the same place, to bring or band together" [13, p. 605]. (The KJV translation "standing" is a subsidiary meaning of the last part of the verb, ἵστημι (*histemi*); the translation does nothing with the prefix σύν (*syn*), which adds the important qualifier "together.") The American Standard 1901 translates it as "compacted." In the late 1970's this verse suggested to me that the original material God created, the deep, was pure water, which He then transformed into other materials. In Appendix C (section 15) I show how God could produce such transformations by simply letting the gravitational collapse take its normal course. The tremendous compression ("compaction") would raise the temperature, pressure, and density to enormous values. This would first rip the hydrogen and oxygen atoms apart into their constituent elementary particles. Then thermonuclear fusion reactions would occur, producing an intense light in the interior during the first day of creation, and generating many different atomic nuclei. The word *sunistemi* seems to me like an excellent choice of words to describe thermonuclear fusion, because it involves "putting together" or "banding together" the various elementary particles and nuclei (fusion) to make different atomic nuclei.

Here is another line of evidence for the possibility that God transformed water into the other elements of the cosmos: In the early 1980's I based a theory about the origin of planetary magnetic fields on the possibility that the earth and other bodies in the solar system were originally created as pure water. The theory has been remarkably successful, even to the point of correctly predicting the Voyager spaceprobe's measurements of the magnetic fields of the planets Uranus and Neptune [7]. The theory could not work with the present elements composing the solar system bodies, but only with water as the original material. Thus it seems that transformation of water on day one (the modern word is "nucleosynthesis") is a distinct biblical and scientific possibility.

> In the beginning God created the heavens and the earth. And the earth was formless and void ...
> — *Genesis 1:1,2.*

If the "nucleosynthesis" scenario above is correct, then it means that at the instant of creation, the earth was merely a small region of water at the center of a much larger ball of water, the deep. That region had no distinguishing marks and was empty of any other kind of matter. This, I suggest, is the meaning of the much-discussed phrase "formless and void," or in Hebrew, תהו ובהו (*tohu wa-bohu*).

In light of Sections 3 through 11, the heavens and earth God created in verse 1 consisted of: (1) a large, mostly empty space (the heavens of heavens), and (2) a ball of ordinary water more than two light-years in diameter. Item (2) contained within itself what would become (a) the waters above the expanse, (b) another heavens called the expanse and the stars within it, and (c) the earth. Thus the first verse would describe the creation of the raw materials of the whole universe, space and water.

12. EARTH STANDARD TIME

In Appendix C (sections 8,9) I show that if the universe is bounded, then *gravitational time dilation* causes clocks (and all physical processes) to tick at different rates in different places. This means we must consider which set of clocks the Bible is referring to when it makes statements about time. For example, referring back to Section 2, the most straightforward understanding of Exodus 20:11 is that Jehovah made the universe in six ordinary days. But "six days" as measured by which clocks? To answer this, first notice that in Genesis 1:5 God Himself provided a definition of the word "day":

> And God called the light day, and the darkness He called night. And there was evening and there was morning, one day — *Genesis 1:5.*

It sounds like a "day" is a period of light and darkness marked off by the rotation of the earth, or in the case of day one, by the rotation of the deep. I will say more about this in the following section. Also notice God's purpose in making the heavenly bodies:

> Then God said, "Let there be lights in the expanse of the heavens to separate the day from the night, and let them be for signs, and for seasons, and for days and years; and let them be for lights in the expanse of the heavens to give light on the earth"; and it was so — *Genesis 1:14,15.*

His intention, among other things, was to give markers in the sky which would allow us to clearly measure periods of time in terms of the *earth's* rotation and the *earth's* movement around the sun, and thus he further defines "days" and "years." In other words, God quite reasonably tells us periods of time in terms of our own frame of reference, not in terms of some otherworldly frame of reference, as some authors would have it [12]. So Genesis 1, Exodus 20:11, and other passages are telling us that God made the universe in 6 days E.S.T. — Earth Standard Time.

13. DAY ONE

Now that I have laid a biblical foundation in this paper and developed a scientific blueprint in the other (Appendix C), let's try to reconstruct the events of creation week. Many details of my reconstruction at this point are speculative and could be wrong, but it is important to spell out exactly how I am picturing these events. Keep in mind that though I write positively, this picture is always subject to revision. Also, please remember that I am not trying to deny the miraculous elements of creation; I am merely considering how God may have used some of the physical laws He Himself invented. The translations in italics from Genesis chapter 1 are my own.

In the beginning God created the heavens ... These include both the heavens of heavens (the second heavens), and also the expanse (the first heavens), as yet not defined within the deep. *... and the earth. And the earth was without form and void ...* The earth, as I said, is a formless, undefined region within the deep, empty of inhabitant or feature.

... and darkness was on the face of the deep, and the Spirit of God was moving on the face of the waters. At the instant of creation, the deep is a sphere of liquid water more than two light-years in diameter. Electromagnetic and nuclear forces (and thus relativistic effects) are fully operational, allowing fully functioning water molecules with their constituent atoms, electrons and nuclei. The deep is rotating with respect to the Spirit of God, and probably with respect to the space within which it exists, the second heavens. There is no visible light at the surface of the deep.

The deep contains all the mass of the visible universe. Gravity is also functioning, and its great strength allows a clearly-defined interface to exist between the waters and the vacuum of the second heavens. The deep is within a black hole, whose outer boundary, called the "event horizon," is 450 million light-years further out, according to equation (14) in Appendix C. As Appendix C, section 12, shows, strange and significant things happen to time near the event horizon. The intense gravity makes the deep collapse toward the center very rapidly. The rate of collapse is not limited by the speed of light (Appendix C, section 12). As the deep is compressed, it becomes very hot and dense. Descending into the deep, we find that molecules, atoms, nuclei, and even elementary particles are being ripped apart.

And God said, "Let there be light," and there was light. At a certain range of depths, thermonuclear fusion reactions begin, forming heavier nuclei from lighter ones (nucleosynthesis) and liberating huge amounts of energy. An intense light illuminates the interior. As the compression continues, the fusion reactions reach a shallow enough depth to allow light to reach the surface, thus ending the darkness there. The strong gravity causes light leaving the surface to return to it, so light at the surface would be coming from all sides. The deep would have no dark side.

And God saw that the light was good, and God separated the light from the darkness. (This paragraph is the most tentative part of my reconstruction of events.) As the collapse continues, gravity becomes so strong that light can no longer reach the surface, re-darkening it. Psalm 104:2, "Covering Thyself with light as with a cloak," appears to refer to day one. That suggests to me that at this point the Spirit of God, "moving [or 'hovering'] over the surface of the waters" (Genesis 1:2), becomes a light source for the surface, in the same way as He will again become a light source at a future time (Revelation 21:23, 22:5). This would give the deep a bright side and a dark side, thus dividing light from darkness and inscribing "a circle on the face of the waters, at the boundary of light and darkness" (Job 26:10, c.f. Proverbs 8:27).

And there was evening and there was morning, one day. Conservation of angular momentum causes the deep to speed up its rotation as the collapse proceeds, like a twirling ice skater speeding up as she brings in her arms. We can imagine a reference point on the surface rotating around to the dark side and continuing further around to the bright side again, marking off evening and morning. Rough calculations (Appendix C, section 15) show that all of the events from the beginning instant to this point had to take place in a very short time, much less than a year. To calculate the time exactly would go beyond the frontiers of modern relativity, but I suspect that a modern clock (if it could survive) on the surface of the deep would register about 24 hours from the instant of creation to the end of day one.

14. DAYS TWO AND THREE

And God said, "Let there be an expanse in the midst of the waters, and let it separate the waters from the waters." And God made the expanse, and separated the waters which were above the expanse from the waters which were below the expanse. Possibly by direct intervention God increases the cosmological "constant" Λ (the tension of space, Appendix C, section 3) to a large positive value, changing the black hole to a white hole (a black hole running in reverse, Appendix C, section 11) and begins rapidly stretching out space. As I showed in Appendix C (section 6), the expansion is not limited by the speed of light, even in conventional theory. God marks off a large volume, the "expanse," within the deep wherein material would be allowed to pull apart into fragments and clusters as it expanded, but He requires the "waters below" and the "waters above" to stay coherently together:

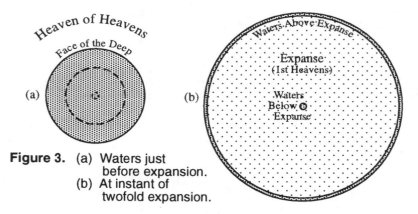

Figure 3. (a) Waters just before expansion.
(b) At instant of twofold expansion.

Normal physical processes cause cooling to proceed as rapidly as the expansion. The stretching of space causes thermal ("heat wave") electromagnetic radiation in the expanse to drop from its initial very high temperature to much lower values in direct proportion to the increase in size of the expanse. These red-shifted heat waves eventually become the cosmic microwave background radiation (Appendix C, section 14). Matter beneath the expanse expands until the surface reaches ordinary temperatures, becoming liquid water underneath an atmosphere. God collects various heavier atoms beneath the surface and constructs minerals of them, laying "the foundations of the earth" (Job 38:4), i.e., its core and mantle. Gravity at the surface drops to normal values. Matter in the expanse is drawn apart into clusters of hydrogen, helium, and other atoms formed by the nucleosynthesis of the first day. The waters above the expanse stay together, becoming thinner as their surface area increases to keep the volume roughly constant. Figure 3(b) illustrates this phase of the expansion.

And God called the expanse "heavens." And there was evening and there was morning, a second day. These heavens are interstellar space, the first heavens as we count outward. The expansion continues at least until the end of the fourth day. Since God has not yet created the sun by this point, the Spirit of God continues to be the light source for the waters below the expanse.

And God said, "Let the waters under the heavens be gathered into one place, and let the dry land appear," and it was so. Rapid radioactive decay and rapid volume cooling occur as secondary effects of the rapid stretching of space (Appendix C, section 15). God uses the radioactivity to heat the continental cratons and to provide power for other geologic work. Thermal expansion makes the cratons buoyant relative to the rocks below them and lifts them above the remaining waters, thus gathering the waters into ocean basins. Volume cooling (a result of the expansion, Appendix C, section 16) solidifies batholiths and much of the athenosphere.

At some time during the expansion, probably on the third day, the waters above the heavens reach the event horizon and pass beyond it. The event horizon (Appendix C, section 11) begins rapidly shrinking toward the earth (Appendix C, section 16). At the same time, gravity draws together the atoms of hydrogen, helium, and other elements in each cluster left behind by the expansion. As Appendix C shows, there has been plenty of time — billions of years — for that process to occur farther out, even though only days have elapsed on earth.

15. THE DAY THE UNIVERSE OPENED (DAY FOUR)
And God said, "Let there be lights in the expanse of the heavens ... to give light on the earth," and it was so. The event horizon reaches earth early in the morning of the fourth day. During that ordinary day as measured on earth, billions of years worth of physical processes take place in the distant cosmos.

And God made the two great lights ... the stars also. And God gave them in the expanse of the heavens to give light on the earth ... Early in the fourth morning, God finishes coalescing the clusters of material left behind in the expansion, and thermo-nuclear fusion begins in the newly-formed stars. During the fourth day the distant stars age billions of years, while their light also has billions of years to travel here. While the light from the more distant galaxies is traveling to earth, space continues to expand, stretching the wavelengths of the light and thus shifting them to the red side of the spectrum (Appendix C, section 14).

And God saw all that He had made, and behold, it was very good. And there was evening and there was morning, the sixth day. God stops the expansion, reducing the cosmological constant Λ to a small positive value or zero, before the evening of the sixth day. Thus Adam and Eve, gazing up for the first time into the new night sky, can now see the Milky Way, the Andromeda galaxy, and all the other splendors in the heavens that declare the glory of God.

16. CONCLUSION
This Bible study has led us to several ideas of profound impor-tance to cosmology:

1. Matter in the universe is bounded.
2. The universe has expanded.

Appendix C shows that, according to the best physics and cosmological knowledge we have today, these ideas lead directly to the conclusion that our cosmos expanded out of a white hole (a black hole running in reverse). As a consequence, gravitational time dilation caused clocks (and all physical processes) both inside and outside the event horizon (the border of the white hole) to tick at vastly different rates from one another in different places. Our Bible study has brought us to several conclusions related to this matter of time:

3. The earth is near the center of the universe.
4. The universe is young as measured by clocks on earth.

Appendix C shows that, given item 3, known physical processes explain item 4, in particular getting light from distant galaxies to us in a short time. Furthermore, the expansion would cause the proper amounts of red shift in light from those galaxies. This Bible study also leads to several other conclusions related to how God formed matter:

5. The original matter God created was ordinary liquid water.
6. God transformed the water into various elements by compaction.

I have suggested, but not proven, here that God did this by the simple means of creating the original waters within a black hole, allowing the resulting rapid gravitational collapse to heat the waters to the point where nucleosynthesis would occur, and finally on the second day converting the black hole to a white hole by beginning the rapid expansion of space. The high temperatures, followed by the expansion, would produce the cosmic microwave background radiation.

I have listed the above conclusions in decreasing order of their cosmological importance and biblical support. These items of vital information from the Bible, as I remarked at the beginning of this paper, lay a good foundation for a young-earth creationist cosmology. The apostle Paul has expressed my feelings about the marvelous subtlety God has shown in making all these things work together in His construction of the universe:

> *O the depth of the riches both of the wisdom and knowledge of God! How unsearchable are his judgments, and his ways past finding out!*
> — Romans 11:33 KJV.

ACKNOWLEDGEMENTS
My hearty thanks to all who have prayed for this project, to the creationist groups and individuals who gave me good biblical feedback and encouragement, to David Rodabaugh, who pointed out several supporting scriptures to me, and to my wife and children for putting up with me all these years of abstraction.

BIBLIOGRAPHY

[1]   F. Brown, *The New Brown-Driver-Briggs-Gesenius Hebrew and English Lexicon*, 1979, Hendrickson Publishers, Peabody, Massachusetts.

[2]   B. Davidson, *The Analytical Hebrew and Chaldee Lexicon*, 1970, Zondervan Publishing House, Grand Rapids. Second edition originally published in 1850 by Samuel Bagster & Sons, Ltd., London

[3]   J. C. Dillow, *The Waters Above: Earth's Pre-Flood Vapor Canopy*, 1981, Moody Press, Chicago.

[4]   J. Green, editor, *The Interlinear Hebrew/Greek English Bible*, Volume I: **Genesis to Ruth**, 1979, Associated Publishers and Authors, Lafayette, Indiana.

[5]   S. W. Hawking and G. F. R. Ellis, *The Large Scale Structure of Space-Time*, 1973, Cambridge University Press, Cambridge.

[6]   W. L. Holladay, editor, *A Concise Hebrew and Aramaic Lexicon of the Old Testament,* 1971, Eerdmans Publishing Company, Grand Rapids. Based on the First, Second, and Third editions of the Koehler-Baumgartner *Lexicon in Veteris Testamenti Libros*.

[7]   D. R. Humphreys, **Good news from Neptune: the Voyager 2 magnetic measurements**, *Creation Research Society Quarterly*, **27:1** 1990, 15-17. Predictions of the Voyager 2 results are in **The creation of planetary magnetic fields**, *Creation Research Society Quarterly*, **21:4** 1984, 140-149.

[8]   D. R. Humphreys, **Progress toward a young-earth relativistic cosmology**, *Proceedings of the Third International Conference on Creationism*, 1994, Creation Science Fellowship, Inc., Pittsburgh.

[9]   K. D. Morrison, **Birds**, *Encyclopedia Americana* **3** (1969) 781-797.

Appendix B

[10]   W. Rindler, *Essential Relativity*, 1977, Revised Second Edition, Springer-Verlag, New York.

[11]   C. C. Ryrie, *The Ryrie Study Bible*, 1978, Moody Press, Chicago.

[12]   G. Schroeder, **The universe — 6 days and 13 billion years old**, *Jerusalem Post*, September 7, 1991. Schroeder has God's clocks ticking off only 6 days of time at the edge of the universe, while earth is 13 billion years old — the reverse of what the equations in my astrophysical paper (Appendix C, section 9) say!

[13]   J. H. Thayer, *Thayer's Greek-English Lexicon of the New Testament*, 1889, Associated Publishers and Authors, Grand Rapids.

[14]   R. E. Walsh, **Biblical hermeneutics and creation**, in *Proceedings of the International Conference on Creationism*, 1987, R.E. Walsh, et al, Editors, Creation Science Fellowship, Pittsburgh, Vol. 1, pp.121-27.

[15]   J. C. Whitcomb, Jr., and H. M. Morris, *The Genesis Flood*, 1961, Baker Book House, Grand Rapids.

[16]   C. J. Yapp and H. Poths, **Ancient atmospheric CO_2 pressures inferred from natural goethites**, *Nature* **355** (23 January 1992) 342-344. The authors' result is that the partial pressure of CO_2 when the Ordovician strata were being laid down was at least 16 times greater than today.

Appendix C

PROGRESS TOWARD
A YOUNG-EARTH RELATIVISTIC COSMOLOGY

D. RUSSELL HUMPHREYS, Ph.D.
Creation Science Fellowship of New Mexico,
P.O. Box 10550, Albuquerque, NM 87184

ABSTRACT
Another paper (Appendix B) of mine at this conference shows evidence that the biblical cosmos has finite boundaries, and that our earth is near the center. If we put those boundary conditions into the equations of Einstein's general theory of relativity, we get an expanding cosmos in which clocks (and all physical processes) tick at different rates in different parts of the universe. The physics is that of a universe-sized "white hole" (a black hole running in reverse), with a shrinking event horizon and matter expanding out of it. At the event horizon, clocks would be momentarily stopped relative to clocks further out. At one critical moment of the expansion, the event horizon would reach the earth, and clocks there would also momentarily stop.

I propose that the critical moment arrived on earth during the fourth day of creation. During that day, billions of years would elapse in the distant sky, allowing light from galaxies to reach the earth within one ordinary day of earth's time. This theory also explains the red shifts of galaxies and the cosmic microwave background. As measured by clocks on earth, the age of the universe today could be as small as the face-value biblical age of about 6000 years.

KEYWORDS
Cosmology, general relativity, age of universe, galactic red shifts, cosmic microwave background, black holes.

1. INTRODUCTION

> *O God! I could be bounded in a nutshell, and count myself a king of infinite space, were it not that I have bad dreams* — Hamlet, Act II.

Appendix C

God used relativity to make a young universe!   That idea, the main thesis of this paper, may seem startling to many people, some of whom may regard relativity as an invention of the devil. But I am proposing here that God invented relativity as an essential part of His universe, and that one feature of relativity in particular, called *gravitational time dilation* by some authors, enabled light from distant galaxies to get to earth in a very short time — within one ordinary day, as measured by clocks here on earth.

People having philosophical problems with relativity may be interested to know that it is possible to separate the mathematics of the theory itself from the philosophical "baggage" so often attached to it, and that a simple conceptual model can do away with the paradoxes people often object to. For example, few people know that Einstein himself came back to the idea of a luminiferous ether in 1920 [15, pp. 13, 23]. The speed of light would be constant with respect to such an ether, and then the equations of relativity would require that clocks and measuring rods moving with respect to the ether change in such a way as to give the same number for the speed of light every time. I.e., objects moving through the ether would be changed by that motion. Clocks would actually slow down, measuring rods would actually shorten, and the speed of light would seem to be independent of motion [39, p.7]. By re-affirming an absolute reference frame, this view of relativity dumps the philosophical baggage and resolves the paradoxes. Section 15 briefly discusses why we might expect relativity to be in operation very early during creation week.

I hope this paper will help convince some of the doubters that relativity is not an enemy of creationism, but is instead a friend. Young-earth creationism needs friends in the area of cosmology, because up to this time, in my opinion, we have had no scientifically satisfactory explanation of the large-scale phenomena we observe in the heavens. The most important of those phenomena are:

1. **Light from distant galaxies** — We see light from galaxies which are billions of light-years away, as measured by a variety of techniques. Light traveling such great distances at today's speed would take billions of years to reach us.

2. **Galactic red shifts** — The wavelengths of light from each galaxy are shifted toward the red side of the spectrum by a factor roughly proportional to the distance of the galaxy from us. There are some exceptions, but the overall trend is very clear and must be explained.

3. **Cosmic microwave background** — The earth is immersed in a bath of low-power microwave (centimeter to millimeter wavelength) electromagnetic radiation whose spectrum is exactly like that of the thermal radiation (heat waves, black-body radiation) found within a cavity whose walls are very cold, at 2.74 Kelvin. After correction for the earth's motion through space, this radiation is very uniform, having variations with direction no greater than one part in 100,000.

All of these phenomena fit reasonably well into the "big-bang" cosmologies, and as such seem to point to a long time scale, billions of years, for the cosmos. Yet creationist scientists have found a great deal of evidence pointing to a very short time scale, much less than millions of years, for the earth and solar system. Good science requires that we try to reconcile both the young-earth data and the cosmological data, thus motivating a creationist cosmology to explain the above phenomena.

In the past, creationists have proposed several such explanations. The most prominent of these are: (*i*) the mature creation theory (light created in transit) [51, p. 369] [49, pp. 222-223] [11, pp. 88-89], (*ii*) the Moon-Spencer theory (shortcut for light) [33] [2] [7], (*iii*) the Setterfield *c*-decay theory (decrease in speed of light) [35] [16] [8], and (*iv*) the Akridge-Barnes-Slusher theory (heating of galactic gas and dust) [2]. All of these theories seem inadequate to me. First, their proponents cite no decisive biblical support. By "decisive" I mean direct statements in the Bible which would clearly favor one theory over another; for example, statements that God created the light in transit, or made it take a shortcut, or speeded it up.

Second, none of these theories explains all three of the large-scale astronomical phenomena listed above. Theories (*i*) through (*iii*) seek mainly to explain light transit time. Theory (*iv*) seeks only to explain the cosmic microwave background. Third, each has severe scientific deficiencies. Theory (*i*) makes no scientific predictions and therefore cannot be checked. Theories (*ii*) through (*iv*) appear to many creationist scientists to have been falsified by the data, although a few remaining advocates of each theory might still disagree. Thus it appears that creationists have not yet produced a satisfactory cosmology.

To meet that need, this paper delves deeply into Einstein's general theory of relativity, going well beyond the special theory of relativity which marks the limit of most physicists' training. It will involve the strange physics of black holes, and it will be rather mathematical. The subject itself requires these things, but I will try to simplify matters as much as possible. For non-physicists I will explain the essential equations in words. For physicists without training in general relativity, I will include concepts that I found helpful as I learned the topic, but such comments may not be very helpful to the non-physicist. I ask you to please bear with me in all these esoterica, because the reward will be great — a non *ad hoc* cosmology which explains the large-scale astronomical phenomena and yet is fully consistent with a young earth.

2. BIG-BANG THEORIES ASSUME AN UNBOUNDED COSMOS

In their book *The Large Scale Structure of Space-Time*, Stephen Hawking and George Ellis [24; p.134] spell out the most fundamental assumption of the modern big-bang cosmologies:

> However we are not able to make cosmological models without some admixture of ideology. In the earliest cosmologies, man placed himself in a commanding position at the centre of the universe. Since the time of Copernicus we have been steadily demoted to a medium sized planet going round a medium sized star on the outer edge of a fairly average galaxy, which is itself simply one of a local group of galaxies. Indeed we are now so democratic that we would not claim our position in space is specially distinguished in any way. We shall, following Bondi [5], call this assumption the *Copernican principle*.

A reasonable interpretation of this somewhat vague principle is to understand it as implying that, when viewed on a suitable scale, the universe is approximately spatially homogeneous.

By "homogeneous," Hawking and Ellis mean that all parts of the universe at any given time are essentially the same. In particular, they mean that all sections of the 3-dimensional space we live in have about the same average matter density ρ, provided that the sections are big enough to allow a good average. This same assumption is fundamental to a larger class of theories called Friedmann, or Robertson-Walker, cosmologies. These include not only the big-bang theories, but also older theories such as Einstein's static cosmos and DeSitter's empty expanding cosmos. Even Fred Hoyle's steady-state cosmology makes the same assumption — homogeneity throughout space. An older name for this "Copernican principle" is the "Cosmological principle."

Notice that Hawking and Ellis call the Copernican principle an "admixture of ideology." By this they mean that it does not come from direct observation but instead from a body of ideas that some people feel to be true. In a recent article in *Nature* [20], astrophysicist Richard Gott spells out the essential reasoning behind the principle:

> In astronomy, the Copernican principle works because, of all the places for intelligent observers to be, there are by definition only a few special places and many nonspecial places, so you are likely to be in a nonspecial place.

To clarify this reasoning further, the idea behind the Copernican principle is that we are on this planet as the result of random processes only — not because of the choice of a purposeful God — and thus it would be unlikely we are in a special place. Of course, this idea of randomness is the essence of Darwinism. Richard Gott noted this connection with evolutionary ideas to build his case that we are not in a privileged location:

> Darwin showed that, in terms of origin, we are not privileged above other species.

So the essential idea behind the Copernican principle is that of a universe ruled by randomness. Since many scientists see a great deal of purpose in nature, there is good reason to question the validity of that principle.

Supporters of the Copernican principle do not rest completely on ideology. They do point out that on a large scale, the universe appears *isotropic* from our point of view. That is, it looks pretty much the same in every direction, especially when we look at the cosmic microwave background. This observed isotropy could indeed result from homogeneity, and thus it is consistent with the Copernican principle. However, logic does not require the reverse line of reasoning — homogeneity as a result of isotropy. In this paper I will show by example that one can conceive of a universe which is isotropic from our viewpoint but not homogeneous.

I have spent some time on the Copernican principle because it has a profound effect on cosmological theory. Richard Gott underlines its importance:

> The idea that we are not located in a special
> spatial location has been crucial in cosmology,
> leading directly to the homogeneous and isotropic
> Friedmann cosmological models ...

You may be wondering at this point what it is about the Copernican principle, or spatial homogeneity, that makes it "crucial." To help you understand, let me spell out clearly an implication of homogeneity which often goes unstated: Homogeneity would mean that our 3-dimensional universe would have *no edges and no center!* If there were an edge or center, observers near those places would be special; they would see and measure different things from other observers, thus violating the Copernican principle.

Suppose you were able to travel instantly to any place in our 3-dimensional space. The Copernican principle says that no matter how far you might travel, you could never find a point where the average mass density ρ is much different from here. You would never encounter an end to the conventional universe of stars and galaxies. There would be no edges or boundaries. In more technical terms, matter in that sort of cosmos is required to be *unbounded*. Mathematicians call this kind of requirement a "boundary condition." Section 4 shows how this boundary condition, when applied to the equations of general relativity, results in the big-bang cosmologies. Section 3 below is an introduction for physicists to the essentials of general relativity. People less mathematically inclined can skip sections 3 and 4 without great loss of understanding.

3. BASICS OF GENERAL RELATIVITY

In 1916, eleven years after his first paper on special relativity, Albert Einstein presented his completed general theory of relativity [13]. In it he pictured space and time as being like a material which is stretched and bent by the presence of mass. Some authors resist this "geometrical" and material interpretation of space [48, p. 147] [50, p. 34], but I prefer it for two reasons: (1) it provides a heuristic picture for an otherwise very difficult subject, and (2) there are some biblical hints favoring it (Appendix B, section 7). Einstein described the stretching and bending by specifying the *interval* between two events occurring at slightly different points in space and time. The interval ds is defined such that if it is a real number, it is proportional to the "natural time" or *proper time* interval $d\tau$ registered by a physical clock as it travels on a trajectory between the two events:

$$ds \equiv c \; d\tau \tag{1}$$

In the system of units I am using, the proportionality factor is the speed of light, c. (If ds is an imaginary number, i.e., if $ds^2 < 0$, then the interval is equal to i times the distance between the two events in a reference frame where they are simultaneous. Some authors define the interval with an opposite sign convention.) Einstein specified the square of the interval by means of an equation called the *metric*:

$$ds^2 = g_{\mu\nu} \, dx^\mu \, dx^\nu, \quad \mu, \nu = 0, 1, 2, 3 \tag{2}$$

The indices μ and ν run from 0 through 3, representing time and the three space dimensions respectively. The four quantities dx^μ represent the distances in time and space between the two events. For example, calling time τ and using polar coordinates (r, θ, ϕ) we might have $(dx^0, dx^1, dx^2, dx^3) = (d\tau, dr, d\theta, d\phi)$. The quantity $g_{\mu\nu}$ represents the $\mu\nu$th component of the *metric tensor*.

Appendix C

In four dimensions, a ("second-rank") tensor is a set of 16 numbers which transform in certain ways when you change coordinate systems. Subscripted indices represent "covariant" tensors, which transform like the derivatives of a scalar function. Superscripted indices represent "contravariant" tensors, which transform like vectors. This equation has both types of tensor, with the metric tensor being in its covariant form and the distances being in their contravariant form. In his paper Einstein introduced his *summation convention*: if you see the same index repeated as both a superscript and subscript, then sum over that index. For example, this means that the right side of eq. (2) represents the sum of 16 different terms. The metric tensor $g_{\mu\nu}$ is fundamentally important in general relativity.

The major contribution in Einstein's 1916 and 1917 [12] papers was his set of 16 gravitational field equations

$$R^{\mu\nu} = \Lambda g^{\mu\nu} - \frac{8\,\pi\,G}{c^4}\left(T^{\mu\nu} - \tfrac{1}{2}g^{\mu\nu}\,T\right) \qquad (3)$$

which govern the curvature (see section 5) of spacetime [39, p. 180]. Put very simply, these equations say that the amount of matter at a given point in spacetime determines the curvature of spacetime at that point. There is a deep similarity to the equations governing a stretched membrane with weights on it, except that here the membrane has four dimensions instead of two. The quantity $R^{\mu\nu}$ on the left side of (3) represents the $\mu\nu$th component of the *Ricci* tensor, which contains various second-order time and space derivatives of the metric tensor. The Ricci tensor is related to the curvature of spacetime [19, p. 39]. In some simple situations it reduces to the D'Alembertian operator

$$\Box \equiv \nabla^2 - \frac{1}{c^2}\frac{\partial^2}{\partial \tau^2} \equiv \frac{\partial^2}{\partial x^2} + \frac{\partial^2}{\partial y^2} + \frac{\partial^2}{\partial z^2} - \frac{1}{c^2}\frac{\partial^2}{\partial \tau^2}$$

applied to the components of the metric tensor [39, pp. 181,190]. In simple static situations, it reduces further to the Laplacian operator ∇^2 applied to the metric components.

On the right side of eq. (3), Λ is the famous "cosmological constant," which can be interpreted as being proportional to an external pressure or tension applied to the membrane of spacetime. (It does not really have to be a constant, but can depend on position or time; nevertheless, most studies keep it a constant, usually zero.) G is the Newtonian gravitational constant.

The second tensor $T^{\mu\nu}$ on the right side of eq. (3) is the *energy-momentum* tensor. It is a "source term" specifying how much mass-energy and momentum (due to non-gravitational fields) are present, causing distortions in spacetime. The third term of eq. (3) contains a scalar function T, which is simply the sum $g_{\mu\nu} T^{\mu\nu}$. The third term represents an additional mass-energy present because of the interaction of the gravitational field with the non-gravitational mass, and it, too, distorts spacetime.

4. FROM GENERAL RELATIVITY TO BIG-BANG COSMOLOGY

The usual approach in cosmology is to figure out first what form the energy-momentum tensor $T^{\mu\nu}$ should have throughout space, and then to find out what form the metric tensor $g_{\mu\nu}$ in eq. (2) must have in order to satisfy the resulting Einstein equations (3). Often cosmologists make two (reasonable) simplifying approximations: (*i*) treat the galaxies as non-interacting "dust," i.e., as if they are too far apart to interact significantly, and (*ii*) assume the galaxies are at rest with respect to space locally; i.e., their only motions are due to the expansion of space. With those approximations the only non-zero component of the energy-momentum tensor is the mass density ρ [39, p. 226]:

$$T^{00} = \rho \qquad (4)$$

Here's where the Copernican principle enters the equations. The principle requires that the mass density ρ in eq. (4) be independent of the space coordinates, *throughout all available space*. Using that boundary condition, many textbooks show that the following metric [48, p. 412], usually called the *Robertson-Walker* metric, is a solution of eq. (3):

$$ds^2 = c^2 \, d\tau^2 - a^2 \left(\frac{d\eta^2}{1 - k \, \eta^2} + \eta^2 \, d\Omega^2 \right) \qquad (5)$$

Here η is a dimensionless radial coordinate. It is a *co-moving* coordinate, meaning the coordinate system moves with the expansion of space, as if it were a grid somehow painted onto space itself. That means for any given galaxy, η will remain the same throughout the expansion. Please note: in the Robertson-Walker metric, the origin of coordinates is completely arbitrary. It can be anywhere in our 3-dimensional space. Thus this metric is fully consistent with the Copernican principle.

The "cosmic" time τ in the Robertson-Walker metric is same as the proper time or "natural" time in eq. (1). It is the time measured by a set of clocks throughout the universe, each one riding with a galaxy as it moves with the expansion of space. These clocks can all be synchronized with one another. Later on I will introduce a distinctly different time, t, often called *Schwarzschild time*, or "coordinate" time. The difference between these two types of time measurements constitutes the essence of this paper, so stay alert for the distinctions.

The symbol a in eq. (5) is the *radius of curvature* of space and has units of distance; it depends on the cosmic time τ. (Some authors define a to be dimensionless and call it the "scale factor"; η would then have units of distance.) The radius of curvature relates the co-moving coordinate η with a radial coordinate r which is not co-moving:

$$r = a(\tau)\, \eta \tag{6}$$

The coordinate r has units of distance and is defined such that the circumference of a circle of radius r is $2\pi r$. For a particular galaxy, r increases as the radius of curvature increases, whereas η remains the same.

The symbol c in eq. (5) represents the speed of light, which is constant in the (τ, r) system for $k = 0$ or near the origin. In other coordinate systems — such as the Schwarzschild system I will introduce later — the speed of light can be c times a function of space and time and therefore not constant. In such systems c by itself does not represent the speed of light but is merely a convenient multiplying constant. (Very often general relativists use physical units such that $c = 1$.) The symbol $d\Omega$ in eq. (5) is the angle subtended, in spherical coordinates, by the two spacetime events defining the interval, so that we have:

$$d\Omega^2 \equiv d\theta^2 + \sin^2\theta \ d\phi^2$$

The constant k in the Robertson-Walker metric is very important. It can have the values 1, 0, or −1, depending on whether the space being described has, respectively, a positive, zero, or negative curvature. When $k = 1$, η has values between 0 and 1. I will try to clarify this concept of curvature in the next section.

5. CURVED SPACE AND *FIVE* DIMENSIONS

The above equations and ideas use four dimensions, one of time and three of space. They are rather mystifying to the newcomer, especially the idea that space might be curved. He asks a very natural question: "What direction could space be curved *toward*?" One of the trade secrets of general relativity is that we can answer this question if we grant admission to the idea of at least one more dimension. In particular, eq. (5) for the case of positive curvature ($k = 1$) has a rather neat geometrical interpretation: our 3-dimensional space would be merely the surface of a "hypersphere" existing in a "hyperspace" having ordinary geometric laws — except that it would have four space dimensions instead of three! Light and all physically observable matter would be confined to moving in the surface. Time would be an extra dimension, a fifth dimension, dealt with separately. To be explicit, the surface of this hypersphere would have Cartesian coordinates (w, x, y, z) such that:

$$w^2 + x^2 + y^2 + z^2 = a^2$$

where a is the radius of curvature in eq. (5). Except for the extra dimension w, this is identical to the equation for a 3-dimensional sphere of radius a. Modern relativists say the hypersphere is a "3-sphere [since its surface is 3-dimensional] embedded [existing] in a Euclidian [ordinary geometry] space of 4 [space] dimensions" [31, p. 704]. Since the radius a increases with time, we can think of the hypersphere as a four-dimensional rubber balloon being inflated. Galaxies would be like pennies pasted on the surface of the balloon; they would all be spreading apart as we inflate the balloon. Many textbooks use this example, but most of them neglect to tell the reader that the balloon has four✳ space dimensions.

Figure 1 shows how equation (5) with $k = 1$ and equation (6) relate to this concept. As I mentioned before, the location of the origin (through which we put the w axis) on the surface of the hypersphere is completely arbitrary. The angle θ represents the amount of rotation around the w axis; the angle ϕ is suppressed. The figure shows three ways to specify the radial distance of a galaxy from the origin: the angle χ or the radial coordinate η (both of which are co-moving), or the radial coordinate r (which is not co-moving).

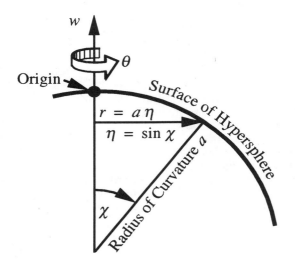

Figure 1. Positive-curvature cosmos

This hyperspherical cosmos may seem like science fiction, but it was Einstein who introduced the concept into cosmology in 1917 [12, p. 185, eq. (10)], using the equation at the beginning of this section with different notation. However, he quickly performed some mathematical sleight-of-hand and swept the extra space dimension w under the rug, so that it was no longer explicit in the equations. Since then, most relativists try to regard it as a convenient mathematical fiction [29, p. 360]. Some, like John A. Wheeler [31, p. 704], even seem rather antagonistic to the possibility of the extra dimension being real:

> Excursion off the sphere is physically meaningless and is forbidden. The superfluous dimension is added to help the reason in reasoning, not to help the traveler in traveling.

Possibly some of this antagonism stems from a distaste for certain 19th-century ideas, either those of the spiritualists, who seized upon hyperspace as a place for ghosts to inhabit, or those of some Christians, who imagined hyperspace as the dwelling place of God. Most likely, it stems from a desire to have the 3-dimensional universe of matter and energy be all of what exists, not merely a part of a much larger reality. Carl Sagan [42, p. 4] expressed this desire as if it were either a definition or a fact:

> The cosmos is all that is or ever was or ever will be.

Creationists, on the other hand, need not be adverse to the possibility of a reality larger than the visible universe, particularly since there are biblical hints of an extra dimension (Appendix B, section 7). One of the difficulties, of course, is being able to visualize or imagine an extra dimension. One help in that regard is Rudy Rucker's mind-stretching little book, *The Fourth Dimension* [41]. Rucker's amusing illustrations and unabashed romps in the fields of speculation make his book an enjoyable introduction to these ideas for both lay person and scientist.

Thus far I have discussed only the case of positive curvature, $k = 1$. We can also visualize the case of zero curvature, $k = 0$, with an extra dimension. In this case, our 3-dimensional space would be the surface of a flat sheet (thin in the w direction) of rubber in a four-dimensional space. Again we glue pennies to the sheet to represent the galaxies, and we represent the expansion by stretching the sheet in the x, y, and z directions. Figures 2 and 3 illustrate the $k = 1$ and $k = 0$ cases by including the w-axis and suppressing the z-axis.

For the case of negative curvature, $k = -1$, we would have a saddle-shaped rubber sheet instead of a flat one. None of these universes has an edge or boundary for the matter in them. The positive-curvature universe has a finite size. If you could travel far enough in one direction (being confined to the surface of the hypersphere), you would eventually come back to your starting point. This feature makes it a *closed* cosmos. But in your travels you would never reach an edge to the stars and galaxies in it (since the matter is spread uniformly over the surface of the hypersphere), making it an *unbounded* cosmos. Thus the positive-curvature Robertson-Walker cosmos would be closed and finite, but unbounded.

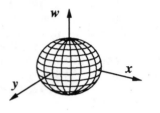

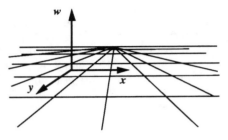

Figure 2. Positive-curvature cosmos

Figure 3. Zero-curvature cosmos

The zero- and negative-curvature (flat and saddle-shaped) universes are not finite. In them, if you traveled in one direction, you could never come back to your starting point. Yet you would never encounter an edge to matter, since the matter in them extends out to infinity. These two kinds of universe would be *open* and unbounded. Thus *all Robertson-Walker (including big-bang) cosmologies have unbounded matter.*

6. MAJOR MISCONCEPTIONS ABOUT BIG-BANG THEORY

At this point we have enough background to grapple with some very common misconceptions. Most people, including most scientists, think that big-bang theorists picture a small sphere of matter exploding outward in a large, pre-existing, empty 3-dimensional space. The outer edge of the exploding matter would then be a boundary between the matter and the empty space surrounding it. But the public's picture of the big bang is wrong! In the case of the closed universe, big-bang mathematics actually says that our 3-dimensional space itself was as small as the matter. Then our 3-dimensional space expanded along with the matter. In other words, big-bang theorists imagine that in the beginning the radius a of their four-dimensional balloon was very small, but that *even then, matter was uniformly distributed along its surface*, and so matter would have no boundary in 3-dimensional space. Journalist Timothy Ferris [17] thinks that the public misconception on this point stems from the name "big bang" itself, which was originally a derogatory label the theory's opponents stuck on it:

> The term "big bang" is misleading in several respects. It implies that the expansion of the universe involved matter and energy exploding like a bomb into preexisting space. Actually the theory depicts all matter, energy, and space-time as having been bound up in the infant, high-density universe. Then, as now, all space was contained in the cosmos, even when the cosmos was smaller than an atom.

However, some of the blame for the public confusion should rest on popularizers like Ferris himself, who neglects to tell his readers that his word "space" really means the 3-dimensional space we inhabit, and who withholds from them the clarifying concept of another space dimension. Also he doesn't say that his words apply only to the positive-curvature versions of big-bang theories. For the zero- and negative-curvature (open) cases, big-bang mathematics actually says that in the beginning space and matter were infinitely large, and matter everywhere had a very high density and temperature. I.e., even at the beginning, the size and mass of the universe would be *infinite*. If in the beginning you had drawn a circle on the flat or saddle-shaped sheets, the circle would get larger as the expansion proceeded, while the density and temperature would get smaller. In other words, the open versions of the big-bang universes start infinitely large and get larger! I can understand why the popularizers are reluctant to explain these concepts to the public.

Two other misconceptions stem from the primary misconception I have mentioned above. The first is that there would be gravitational forces pointing toward the assumed center of the big bang. The second is that those assumed forces would be so strong that the initial phases of the big bang would be in a black hole (I will say much more about black holes later). But in the actual big-bang theory there is no center in 3-dimensional space for gravitational forces to point to. Every point in 3-dimensional space would have, on the average, an equal amount of matter at large distances in all directions from the point. So the overall gravitational force on each point due to the surrounding universe would be zero. (Of course the gravitational forces from nearby objects, such as our own planet, would not be zero but quite substantial.) Because of this cancellation, no large-scale pattern of gravitational forces would exist, and so a big-bang cosmos could never be in a black hole.

A fourth misconception is that no galaxy could move away from us faster than the speed of light. But many books on standard cosmology [46, pp. 148-149] point out that for every point in our 3-D space there is a "horizon" beyond which the recession velocity would exceed the speed of light, and that galaxies should exist beyond that horizon. However, at the horizon, the red shift would be infinitely large, and it would be impossible for us to see beyond it. In cosmology, matter cannot move through our 3-D space faster than the locally-measured speed of light, but *space itself* is not limited that way. (Some authors [see section 3] dislike, for philosophical reasons, this picture of space itself expanding, but they offer no alternative picture to help explain the distinctions.) For example, going back to Fig. 1, matter and light waves can only move along (or in) the surface of the hypersphere, and they cannot move faster than c with respect to the surface in their vicinity. But the surface itself can move radially outward faster than the speed of light, and according to the $k = 1$ version of big-bang theory, it is doing so right now. In fact, Alan Guth's "inflationary" version of big-bang cosmology [21] has the hypersphere, during an early phase of its expansion, increasing its radius a at 10^{20} times the speed of light!

A fifth misconception is that the red shifts of the galaxies are Doppler shifts, i.e. caused by the velocity of the galaxies away from us at the time the light starts its journey toward us. But one undergraduate textbook [23, pp. 236, 245-246] and many graduate textbooks [39, p. 213] make it clear that the red shifts are an *expansion* effect. As space is stretched out, the lengths of all electromagnetic waves passing through the space are similarly stretched out. Consequently, the *speed* of recession doesn't matter, only the *amount* of expansion that takes place as the light travels to us, whether the expansion is fast or slow. Somehow this distinction has escaped even most physicists, unless they are specialists in general relativity. I will say more about this in Section 14.

In summary, the widely accepted big-bang cosmologies have five little-known features which are very important to understand here:

1. *Matter in the universe never had any bound- aries, has none now, and never will.*
2. *There is no large-scale pattern of centrally- directed gravitational forces.*
3. *The universe never was in a black hole.*
4. *Space can expand faster than the speed of light.*
5. *The red shifts are not Doppler shifts.*

It is ironic that so many enthusiastic supporters of the big bang are completely ignorant of these basic features of the theory they promote.

7. REASONS TO CONSIDER A BOUNDED COSMOS

Section 2 shows that the Copernican principle is an entirely arbitrary assumption, an "admixture of ideology" as Hawking and Ellis put it. Therefore it makes scientific sense to explore the consequences of the opposite assumption, a bounded universe. The matter in such a universe would not occupy all the available 3-dimensional space, but instead there would be empty space beyond the matter.

Appendix B, "A Biblical Basis for Creationist Cosmology," concludes that:

1. **The cosmos is bounded** — Interstellar space, the ordinary heavens of stars and galaxies, has a finite (though very large) size and a definite boundary. Beyond it are "the waters above the heavens," of undetermined thick- ness. For some unspecified distance beyond those waters there exists more space of the same sort as interstellar space, but empty of matter.

2. **The earth is near the center** — Interstellar space has a center of mass, and the earth is "near" it by cosmic standards, meaning the present distance between the earth and the center is small compared to billions of light- years.

3. **The cosmos has been expanded** — God "stretched out" interstellar space at some time in the past, probably during creation week. Space may or may not be expanding now.

4. **The cosmos is young** — God created the universe in six earth days, i.e., in six ordinary rotation periods of our particular planet.

Appendix B offers evidence that, of all the known ways to understand the relevant scriptures, these are the most straightforward. If that is true, then it should be clear that these are not *ad hoc* assumptions, invented only recently to solve cosmological problems — because the Bible greatly predates our awareness of those problems. Thus these conclusions provide a very reasonable "admixture of ideology" to build our cosmological models upon. Conclusions 1 and 2 are the most important ones to our discussion right now. They are essentially the opposite of the Copernican principle, and so fit our scientific motivation to see what a non-Copernican cosmology would be like.

8. GRAVITY IN A BOUNDED COSMOS

Let us now see what differences boundaries make. First of all, the existence of boundaries requires the existence of a center of mass. This means that a large-scale pattern of *gravitational force* must exist throughout the cosmos, everywhere pointing toward the center of mass. If we are near the center, then the fact that the universe looks isotropic (the same in every direction) to us means that the universe must be approximately spherically symmetric. To keep things simple (they are going to get complex enough anyway) for this paper, let's assume (*i*) no overall rotation of the cosmos and (*ii*) that the mass density ρ is constant out to a radius r_0 from the center, and zero beyond that. Also, for this section only, let's ignore the effects of expansion. In that case, the large-scale gravitational force is approximately related to a Newtonian *gravitational potential* Φ [29, p. 298, 1st footnote] which depends on the radius r as follows:

$$\Phi(r) = -2\pi G \rho \left(r_0{}^2 - \tfrac{1}{3} r^2 \right) \text{ for } r \le r_0,$$
$$\text{and } \Phi(r) = -\frac{G\,m}{r} \text{ for } r > r_0, \tag{7}$$

where m is the total mass of the universe,

$$m = \frac{4}{3} \pi \rho r_0^3 \tag{8}$$

(For those not familiar with this concept, gravitational potential is the energy you would need to lift one kilogram of mass from some point at radius r up to a point very far beyond radius r_0, where the gravitational force is essentially zero. It is also one-half the square of the *escape velocity* at that point, which is how fast you would have to throw the mass in order for it to escape the bounds of the universe.) Figure 4 shows how the depth of this gravitational potential "well" decreases with increasing distance r from the center. The slope of the walls of the well gives the gravitational force; the steeper the wall, the greater the force. You can think of this well as being caused by the weight of a mass upon a stretched rubber membrane. The more concentrated the mass, the deeper the well, as Figure 5 shows.

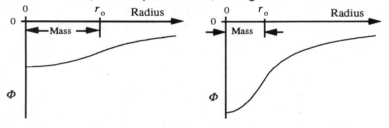

Figure 4. Gravitational potential "well."   **Figure 5.** Well with more concentrated mass.

The earth, being near the center, would be near the bottom of this well, with most of the universe being at a higher (less negative) gravitational potential.

9. GRAVITY SLOWS TIME DOWN
The above differences in gravitational potential from place to place would produce differences in the rates of clocks — and all physical processes. To see this, let's consider an approximate general relativistic metric for this situation [45, p. 185]:

$$ds^2 \approx \left(1 + 2\frac{\Phi}{c^2}\right)c^2\,dt^2 - \left(1 - 2\frac{\Phi}{c^2}\right)(dx^2 + dy^2 + dz^2), \tag{9}$$

where the Cartesian coordinates (x, y, z) are related to the spherical coordinates (r, θ, ϕ) in the usual way. This approximation is good when $|\Phi| << c^2$. Imagine the two events marking off the interval ds as being the successive ticks of a clock which is motionless in this system of coordinates. Since the two ticks take place at the same location in space, the distance differences dx, dy, and dz are all zero. Using that information plus eq. (1) in eq. (9), and taking the positive square root, gives us the following relation between the proper (or "natural") time interval $d\tau$ measured by physical clocks and the time interval dt, which is the *Schwarzschild time* (or "coordinate" time) I warned you to watch out for:

$$d\tau \approx \left(1 + \frac{\Phi}{c^2}\right) dt \qquad (10)$$

Other authors have also derived this equation [29, pp. 248-249]. Notice that when the gravitational potential is zero, the two types of time intervals are equal, so that $d\tau = dt$. This means that Schwarzschild time t is the time measured by a clock which is not in a gravitational field. Far beyond the boundary radius r_0 of the cosmos, the gravitational potential is practically zero, so t is the time registered by very distant clocks. If we could make a set of ideal clocks throughout the universe which were not affected by gravity, we could theoretically synchronize all those clocks with one of the very distant clocks [31, pp. 597]. (One way to make such a set of gravitationally-unaffected clocks would be to let all the clocks in the set fall freely, since by Einstein's equivalence principle and also by experimental observation, free fall is equivalent to zero gravity. Another way, in theory, would be to determine the gravitational potential at every point in space and compensate the clock rates accordingly.) The synchronized set would then measure Schwarzschild time. We could think of the whole set as being "God's clock," an ideal clock completely unaffected by such mundane things as gravity. As such, Schwarzschild time makes a good standard against which we can compare the rates of less ethereal and more variable clocks.

In this light, eq. (10) says that natural, physical, clocks are indeed affected by gravity. Since the gravitational potential Φ has negative values, the equation says that wherever Φ is not zero,

$d\tau$ is less than dt. I.e., clocks in a gravitational field tick slower than clocks which are not in a gravitational field. Moreover, the deeper you go into a gravitational well, the slower physical clocks tick. Although this effect is nearly unknown to the public, many authors in general relativity describe it. Here is a sampling:

> ... it follows that clocks fixed at a lower potential go slower than clocks fixed at a higher potential. This is called "gravitational time dilation" [39, p. 21].

> The rate of a clock is accordingly slower the greater is the mass of the ponderable matter in its neighbourhood [14, p. 92].

> Thus at finite distances from the masses there is a "slowing down" of the time compared with the time at infinity [29, p. 302].

> Clocks go slower in the vicinity of large masses [46, p. 27].

The second quote is by Einstein. This general-relativistic *gravitational time dilation* is not the same as the well-known "velocity" time dilation (slowdown of clocks due to motion) of special relativity. General relativity says that gravity slows down not only clocks, but also *all physical processes*: atoms, nuclei, chemical and biochemical reactions, electromagnetic waves, nerve impulses in your brain, sand in an hourglass, the watch on your arm, rotations and orbits of planets — everything! Thus we would have no direct means of observing this slowdown in our vicinity, because all of the ways we could notice or measure it are also slowed down. The slowdown is *locally* transparent to us; we cannot detect it by measurements just at one place. For example, if we were to measure the speed of light with physical clocks located near the Sun, we would get the same number as we do on earth. However, if we could do the measurements with ideal Schwarzschild clocks, we would find that the speed of light is lower near the Sun. So in general relativity, even the speed of light is affected by gravity [18, p. 23] — if we use the right clocks!

The only previous author I know of who seems to have included something like gravitational time dilation in a cosmology is Gerald L. Schroeder. His article in the *Jerusalem Post* [44] contains few scientific details, but it appears to have clocks ticking fast at the center and slow at the edge of the cosmos — just the reverse of what the equations in this section show. After submitting the first draft (August 30, 1993) of this article, I finally succeeded in contacting him; as far as I can tell from his reply (October 29, 1993), his concepts are quite different from the cosmology I am presenting here.

10. THE SLOWDOWN OF TIME — PRESENT AND PAST
Gravitational time dilation is not mere theory, however. There are ways to measure it, and it has been measured many times. Below are some samples:

1. **Deflection of electromagnetic waves** — Half of the famous deflection of light as it passes the Sun is due to gravitational slowing of the speed of light, the other half coming from the effect of gravity on space. For many years, critics of general relativity correctly pointed out that the solar eclipse measurements of the deflection of starlight were very inaccurate. But in 1975, measurements of radio waves from three quasars as the Sun passed close to them in the sky confirmed Einstein's prediction of the deflection to an accuracy of better than 1% [39, p. 22].

2. **Radar in the solar system** — In 1965, I. I. Shapiro measured the travel times of radar waves passing by the Sun and bouncing back from the planet Venus. The results confirmed the predictions of general relativity, particularly gravitational time dilation, to within 3% [46, pp. 41-45]. A few years later, the travel times of radio signals from the Mariner 6 and 7 spacecraft also confirmed the theory to about the same accuracy.

3. **Atomic clocks in airplanes** — In 1971 Joseph Hafele and Richard Keating flew atomic clocks in eastbound and westbound airline flights, trying to measure the effect of gravitational time dilation due to the change of altitude. After

correcting for velocity time dilation, they con-firmed gravitational time dilation to within 10%. Four years later a team from the University of Maryland did a similar experiment, but more accurately, confirming the predicted time dilation to an accuracy of nearly 1% [46, pp. 29-35].

4. **Atomic clocks on the ground** — Wolfgang Rindler [39, p. 21] reports: "Indeed, owing to this effect [gravitational time dilation], the U.S. atomic standard clock kept since 1969 at the National Bureau of Standards at Boulder, Colorado, at an altitude of 5400 ft, gains about five microseconds per year relative to a similar clock kept at the Royal Greenwich Observatory, England, at an altitude of only 80 ft, both clocks being intrinsically accurate to one microsecond per year."

These and other experiments make it clear that gravitational time dilation is real. However, 5 microseconds/year per mile of altitude difference does not seem like a large effect. How big would the effect be for the whole universe at present? To answer that question we need to determine the gravitational potential $\Phi(0)$ at the center of the universe. Solving eq. (8) for ρ and substituting it into eq. (7) with $r = 0$ gives us the potential at the center in terms of the total mass m and radius r_0 of the universe:

$$\Phi(0) = -\tfrac{3}{2} G \frac{m}{r_0} \qquad (11)$$

Now we need to estimate the radius r_0 and mass density ρ of the universe. The most distant radio galaxies observed are supposed to be about 12 billion light-years away [9], according to the standard cosmological interpretation of their red shifts, so let us try $r_0 = 20$ billion light-years. The observed density of luminous matter in our cosmic neighborhood is on the order of 10^{-28} kg/m^3 [34, pp. 323-329]. Using those numbers in eq. (8) gives us an estimate for the mass of the universe:

$$m \approx 3 \times 10^{51} \quad \text{kg} \qquad (12)$$

Using the mass and radius above in eq. (11) gives us a potential of $-1.7 \times 10^{15} m^2/s^2$ at the center of the universe. Plugging that potential into eq. (10) shows that clocks at the center should presently be ticking only about 2% slower than clocks very far away. So, given the above density and size, clock rates should be about the same throughout today's universe. (Of course, if "dark matter" proves to be substantial or the size of the cosmos is much greater than 20 billion light-years, clock rates would be very different in different parts of the universe even today.)

But what about clock rates in the past? If the universe has indeed expanded, as both the biblical and scientific data indicate, then the radius r_0 of the universe was smaller in the past. That means the potential well would have been deeper than now, as eq. (11) shows and Figure 5 illustrates. In fact, eq. (11) suggests that if r_0 was about fifty times smaller, the depth of the gravitational potential well would have been about c^2. That means the escape velocity [section 8] from a point near the center would have been about the speed of light — so light from the center could not have escaped the universe! Also, using $-c^2$ for the potential in eq. (10) suggests that clocks at the center would have been stopped!

Values of potential as large as c^2 are well beyond the limits ($|\Phi| \ll c^2$) whereby equations (9) and (10) are good approximations. However, it is clear that strange things would have happened to light and time when the universe was smaller. The next section delves into those peculiarities with a more accurate metric.

11. BLACK HOLES AND WHITE HOLES

A month after Einstein published his field equations (3) with $\Lambda=0$, Karl Schwarzschild, a German physicist serving in the Prussian army, found the first exact solution of them [30, p. 119] [29, p. 301, eq. (100.14)], a metric which describes spacetime in the vacuum surrounding a sphere of mass m :

$$ds^2 = \left(1 - \frac{r_s}{r}\right) c^2 \, dt^2 - \frac{dr^2}{1 - \frac{r_s}{r}} - r^2 \, d\Omega^2 , \qquad (13)$$

$$\text{where} \quad r_s \equiv \frac{2 \, G \, m}{c^2}$$

The radial distance r is the same as in eq. (6). The time t is same as the Schwarzschild time defined in the previous section. In

1923, G. D. Birkoff [4] found that the Schwarzschild metric is valid even for contracting or expanding masses, as long as they remain spherically symmetric. The parameter r_s, called the *Schwarzschild radius*, is a critical size of great importance. Using the mass given by eq. (12), the Schwarzschild radius of the universe would be:

$$r_s = 450 \times 10^6 \text{ light-years}, \tag{14}$$

i.e., about a half-billion light-years. Remember that in the previous section we assumed the universe presently has a matter radius r_0 of 20 billion light-years. If in the past the universe were 50 times smaller, all of its matter would be inside its Schwarzschild radius. To understand what this means, we must now discuss *black holes* and *white holes*.

In the mid-1960's John Wheeler applied the term "black hole" to the idea of a collapsing star whose matter has all fallen within its Schwarzschild radius. It turns out that light or matter from such a star can never escape beyond the Schwarzschild radius. The sphere defined by the Schwarzschild radius is called the *event horizon*, because from outside it, you could never see events happening inside it. Light and matter from outside could fall into the event horizon, but nothing could ever return from it — hence the name "black hole." As more and more matter falls into a black hole, its mass increases, and so its event horizon always is moving outward. Jean-Pierre Luminet's book, *Black Holes*, recently translated into English [30], is an excellent introduction to the topic for both laymen and scientists.

There are a few misconceptions about black or white holes we should dispose of here. The first is that in them densities and tidal forces (which try to pull things apart) are always huge. But if you take the mass of eq. (12) and spread it uniformly throughout a sphere whose radius is that of eq. (14), you get a density of only 8×10^{-24} kg/m^3. Tidal forces would also be tiny. If you were to concentrate all the mass into an infinitesimal "singularity" at the very center, then the density would be infinite at that point, but zero everywhere else. Tidal forces near the singularity would be very great, but forces further out would remain small. A black hole has an event horizon long before a singularity forms, and a white hole need not have a singularity except possibly (not necessarily) at the instant of its creation. Thus forces and den-sities aren't necessarily large. The second misconception is that black holes are black inside. But light can and probably does exist within them. We just can't see it from outside the event horizon.

There is good astronomical evidence that black holes actually exist [30, pp. 250-252]. Astronomers have identified three objects in the sky which emit x-rays of the sort which matter falling into a black hole would emit: Cygnus X-1, LMC X-3, and A 0620-00. Each of these is a double star system, with a visible star orbiting an invisible companion. The mass of each of the companions appears to be well above 3 solar masses, the theoretical limit to the mass a compact star can have without collapsing into a black hole.

The same equations which describe a black hole also allow for the existence of an "anti-black hole" or *white hole*, the term some astrophysicists use for the idea of a black hole running in reverse. A white hole would expel matter out of its event horizon instead of pulling matter into it. Light (and matter) would leave the white hole, but no light (or matter) could go back in. As matter leaves the white hole, its mass decreases, so its event horizon would move inward. Eventually the event horizon would reach radius zero and disappear, leaving behind a widely-distributed collection of ordinary matter. The term "white hole" never really became popular, perhaps because such an object would be a source, not a "hole." Luminet suggests the poetic name "white fountain" [30, p. 165]. I like that term, but as yet it has not become familiar enough to be useful.

Matter cannot sit still inside an event horizon [29, p. 311]. In a black hole, matter *must* move inward; in a white hole, matter *must* move outward.

There is no evidence as yet that small white holes exist. However, eq. (14) suggests that the *universe* started as a white hole! This conclusion follows directly from boundedness and expansion. Such an origin is quite different from big-bang theories.

12. TIME AND THE EVENT HORIZON

Let's consider what happens to clocks near the event horizon. Again setting dr and $d\Omega$ equal to zero in eq. (13), using eq. (1), and taking the positive square root as we did in section 9, we get a relation between proper time $d\tau$ and Schwarzschild time dt:

$$d\tau = \sqrt{1 - \frac{r_s}{r}}\, dt\,, \quad \text{for} \quad r > r_s \qquad (15)$$

At great distances outside the event horizon, we again see that the two types of time are the same. As r decreases and gets close to the value r_s, the proper time intervals become much smaller than the Schwarzschild time intervals. Stephen Hawking [25, p. 87] tells the story of a man, say an astronaut, falling toward the event horizon of a large black hole. Here I paraphrase the story as follows:

> The astronaut is scheduled to reach the event horizon at 12:00 noon, as measured by his watch (proper time). An astronomer watching from very far away (thus being on Schwarzschild time) sees the watch tick slower and slower as the astronaut approaches the event horizon, a dark sphere blocking off a starry background. The astronomer sees the watch reach 11:57 a.m. After an hour (of Schwarzschild time) the watch reaches 11:58. After a day (of Schwarzschild time), he sees the watch reach 11:59. The astronomer never does see the watch reach 12:00. Instead he sees the motionless images of the astronaut and his watch getting redder and dimmer at the event horizon, finally fading from view completely.

Hawking doesn't describe very much of what the astronaut sees, so I will take up his story:

> As the astronaut approaches the event horizon, he looks back through a telescope at the astronomer's observatory clock (Schwarzschild time) and sees it running faster and faster. He sees the astronomer moving rapidly around the observatory like a video in fast-forward. He sees planets and stars moving very rapidly in their orbits. The whole universe far

109

away from him is moving at a frenzied pace, aging rapidly. Yet the astronaut sees that his own watch is ticking normally. Finally when the astronaut's watch (proper time) reaches 12:00 noon, he sees that the hands of the astronomer's clock are moving so fast they have become a blur. As he passes the event horizon, he feels no unusual sensations, but now he sees bright light inside the horizon. His watch reaches 12:01 and continues ticking. He looks back toward the astronomer and sees ...

To find out what the astronaut sees next, we must figure out what happens to clocks inside the event horizon. Eq. (15) does not apply when r is less than r_s. But if we consider that inside the event horizon the escape velocity must be greater than the speed of light, then we could say that the gravitational potential Φ must be more negative than $-c^2$. Eq. (10) then suggests (but does not require because of its limits of approximation) that $d\tau$ and dt might have opposite signs — the two types of clocks might *run in opposite directions!*

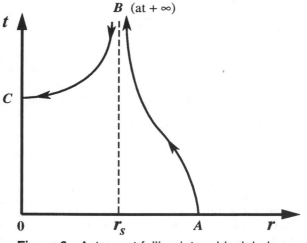

Figure 6. Astronaut falling into a black hole.

It appears to be another "trade secret" of general relativity, unpublicized by the adepts, that black hole theory supports this

110

astonishing possibility. Figure 6 is adapted from a well-respected graduate textbook by John Wheeler and two colleagues, Kip Thorne and Charles Misner [31, p. 825]. It shows how the Schwarzschild time t varies as the astronaut's inward fall decreases the radius r. The arrows show the direction of increasing proper time; that is, the astronaut's watch increases its reading from point A to point B to point C. Although the Schwarzschild time goes to infinity at point B, the proper time τ does not. As the astronaut continues falling past the event horizon, the Schwarzschild time *decreases* (even while the proper time is increasing), all the way to point C. Thus, although the Schwarzschild time goes to infinity at the event horizon, the *net* amount of Schwarzschild time elapsed in going from A to C is finite. The proper time elapsed is also finite, and it is smaller than the net Schwarzschild time elapsed [31, p. 848]. Also notice that the slope of the astronaut's trajectory as it approaches C is nearly zero. This means that as measured in Schwarzschild time, the astronaut's speed is much greater than c and approaches infinity! Wheeler feels that Schwarzschild time is a bad "choice" of coordinates in this case, its "unhappy" features being shown in two ways:

> ... (1) in the fact that t goes to ∞ partway through the motion; and (2) in the fact that t thereafter decreases as τ (not shown) continues to increase.

Wheeler's word "choice" implies that Schwarzschild time is merely a matter of arbitrary theoretical taste, having no particular connection with physical measurements. However, as I pointed out in section 9 in my comments on eq. (10), Schwarzschild time has a clear physical meaning. It tells us the relation between local clocks and clocks at a distance, or between rates of physical processes and clocks unaffected by gravity. For example, it can tell us what the astronaut sees outside the event horizon when he himself is inside it:

> ... and he sees (since light can go inward through the horizon) the astronomer's clock still running so fast that the hands are a blur. As he watches, the hands of the clock slow down enough to let him see that they are moving very rapidly *counter-clockwise*. The huge amount of time he saw the clock record before he crossed the event horizon

is now being taken away. As the astronaut continues inward away from the event horizon, the astronomer's clock slows down toward normal speed, but it is still going backwards. The astronaut's own watch now reads 12:05. He sees the astronomer back away from the telescope and walk backwards toward the door. As far as the astronaut can see, time in the whole universe outside the event horizon is running *backwards*.

A white hole would reverse this fantastic voyage. Figure 7 shows the spacetime path of an astronaut as a white hole expels him out of its event horizon.

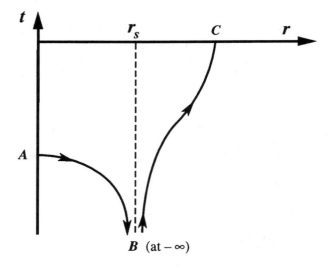

Figure 7. Astronaut expelled out of a white hole.

Light and material from outside cannot move inward through the event horizon, so the astronaut cannot see the outside universe. However, an astronomer outside the event horizon would be able to see the astronaut clearly, since light and material can and do flow out of the event horizon. The arrows again show the direction of increase of proper time, from *A* to *B* to *C*. Again, it only takes a finite amount of proper time for the astronaut to go beyond the event horizon.

Let's say the astronaut is scheduled to cross the event horizon at 12:00 midnight by his watch. Here is his view of events:

As the astronaut begins his journey out of the white hole, there is bright light behind him, but the event horizon looks like a black wall in front of him. As he approaches the wall he glances at his watch; it reads 11:59 p.m. A minute later, as his watch reaches 12:00 midnight, he passes through the event horizon. He feels no particular sensation, but suddenly he sees the whole starry universe outside the event horizon. He can still see the bright light coming from behind. Looking through a telescope at the astronomer's observatory clock, he sees its hands moving very rapidly clockwise, and the astronomer is moving very rapidly around the observatory. Looking elsewhere, the astronaut sees the whole universe moving in fast-forward, aging very rapidly. As the astronaut gets further away from the event horizon, he sees the astronomer's clock slowing down to more normal speeds. As he arrives at the observatory, the astronomer's clock has finally slowed down to the speed of the astronaut's watch.

The astronaut tells the astronomer how fast the astronomer was aging. The astronomer has seen some strange things too, and he tells the astronaut how slowly the astronaut was aging. They argue for a while, and then finally decide that black holes and white holes do strange things to time, especially near the event horizon. But strange as such effects may seem, they are a real possibility, according to our best experimental and theoretical knowledge of physics. If the universe is bounded and has expanded, then these odd "time warps" in the past history of the cosmos are an unavoidable scientific consequence. However, creationists need not try to avoid them, because they work in our favor to allow a young universe.

13. WHAT HAPPENS INSIDE THE MATTER SPHERE
Thus, if the universe is bounded and has expanded, there was a time in its early history when all its matter was well within the event horizon, not yet having expanded to the 450 million light-

years of eq. (14). During that time, the Schwarzschild metric for vacuum, eq. (13), would be valid through all the empty space between the matter and the event horizon, as well as outside it. But at some point in the expansion, the outermost matter would reach the event horizon. After that, matter would be flowing out of the event horizon, and we would expect the event horizon to start shrinking. But to understand properly what happens inside the matter's boundary, we need a different metric than eq. (13). This section will provide such a metric and explore some of its consequences.

By the time the matter reaches the event horizon, we can consider most of it as "dust," that is, the various clusters of matter are far apart enough not to be interacting significantly. Many authors on general relativity deal with the collapse of a uniform sphere of dust to become a black hole [29, pp. 316-321] [48, pp. 342-349]. The same equations apply to our situation of a uniform dustlike sphere expanding out of a white hole, except that all motions run in reverse [29, p. 320]. Therefore we can use the same metric as they derive.

The result of their work is that inside the sphere, the metric is *almost* identical to the Robertson-Walker metric, eq. (5), for $k = 1$. In the co-moving coordinate system (η, τ) of eq. (5), let's define η_0 as the co-moving radial coordinate of the sphere's edge. Then for values $\eta \le \eta_0$, eq.(5) is a valid metric. However there is one very important difference. Whereas for an unbounded Robertson-Walker cosmos, the origin can be anywhere, here the origin of coordinates *must be at the center* of the sphere and nowhere else. But seen from the center of the sphere, many phenomena will be the same as in a Robertson-Walker cosmos.

Outside the sphere, the metric has to be the same as the Schwarzschild metric, eq. (13). Therefore at the edge of the matter, at $r = r_0$ for the Schwarzschild metric and at $\eta = \eta_0$ for the Robertson-Walker metric, the two solutions must coincide. But since the two metrics use different types of coordinates, we must convert one of the metrics to the other set of coordinates. For our purposes we need the metric inside the sphere in terms of the Schwarzschild coordinates (r, t). Only two authors I know of follow that procedure, Steven Weinberg [48, pp. 345-346] and Oskar Klein [28, pp. 67-72]. Klein's interpretation of some of his mathematics is now somewhat outdated; see [29, p. 309-320] for a more recent view. But his mathematics are correct, and his exposition and notation are more suited to our needs. Unfortunately for many people, Klein's article is in German, with no published English translation that I know of. I have translated the relevant sections into English for my own convenience, and I will be happy to make the translation available to anyone who can use it [28].

As Schwarzschild did, Klein sets the cosmological constant Λ equal to zero in Einstein's equations (3). He then obtains a solution in the form of the following metric:

$$ds^2 = \beta\,c^2\,dt^2 - \alpha\,dr^2 - r^2\,d\Omega^2 \qquad (16)$$

where α and β are functions to be specified below. Inside the sphere, for $r \le r_0$, we have:

$$\alpha = \frac{1}{1 - \dfrac{a_0\,r^2}{a^3}}, \quad \text{where} \quad a_0 \equiv \sqrt{\frac{3\,c^2}{8\,\pi\,G\,\rho_0}} \qquad (17a,b)$$

As before, a is the radius of curvature of space, which varies with proper time τ. Under these conditions a will reach a maximum value a_0, which eq (17b) relates to the minimum matter density ρ_0 occurring at the time of maximum a. Equations (6) and (8) are also valid here, so you can use them to get ρ_0 in terms of the total mass m and η_0.

Figure 8 (on the next page) illustrates the geometry of the bounded cosmos described by equations (16) and (17), again using the extra space dimension w and suppressing the angle ϕ. As in Figure 1, the angle θ represents the amount of rotation around the w axis. The radius r_0 shows the edge of the matter distribution, also denoted by the co-moving coordinate η_0. The location of the origin cannot be moved, but must remain at the center of the matter distribution as shown. In all other ways, space inside r_0 is simply a section of the hypersphere shown in Figure 1, corresponding to the Robertson-Walker metric. Inside the sphere, the *proper distance* [48, p. 415, eq. (14.2.21)] along the surface of the hypersphere at any given proper time would be $a\,\chi$.

115

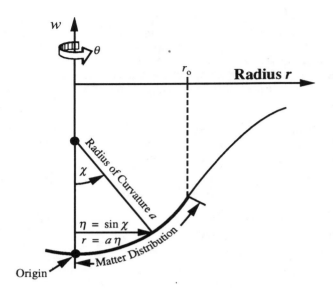

Figure 8. Geometry of bounded cosmos.

Outside of r_0, space corresponds to the Schwarzschild metric. The similarity of Figure 8 to Figure 5 is significant, but only approximate. The other coefficient of eq. (16) is related to time and therefore of more interest to us. It is:

$$\beta = \frac{\left[1 - \frac{a_0}{a}\left(1 - \frac{\left(1 - \eta_0^2\right)^{3/2}}{\left(1 - \eta^2\right)^{1/2}}\right)\right]^2}{\left(1 - \frac{a_0}{a}\eta^2\right)\left[1 - \frac{a_0}{a}\left(1 - \frac{\left(1 - \eta_0^2\right)^{1/2}}{\left(1 - \eta^2\right)^{1/2}}\right)\right]^3} \tag{18}$$

To decipher this rather formidable expression, it may help to remember that η and η_0 are the co-moving radial coordinates of, say, a galaxy and the edge of the sphere, respectively. So for a galaxy, the only variable in this equation that changes with proper time is the radius of curvature a, which is always equal to

116

or less than a_0. Certain combinations of η and a will cause the numerator to be zero, so natural clocks would be stopped at the corresponding radii and times.

Now we need to find out how the radius of curvature a of the sphere of matter depends on proper time τ. For the case of the cosmological constant $\Lambda = 0$, many authors [27, pp. 320,321] derive $a(\tau)$ from the Einstein field equations (3). For my purposes it is easier to use $\tau(a)$:

$$\tau = \pm \frac{\tau_0}{\pi} \left[\operatorname{Arccos}\left(2\frac{a}{a_0} - 1\right) + 2\sqrt{\frac{a}{a_0} - \left(\frac{a}{a_0}\right)^2} \right] , \quad \text{(19a,b)}$$
$$\text{where} \quad \tau_0 \equiv \frac{a_0}{c}$$

where I use the plus sign for a collapsing sphere and a minus sign for an expanding one.

Figure 9. Expansion and contraction of sphere

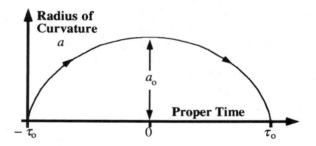

Figure 9 shows the curve traced out by eq. (19), a cycloid. The left side of the curve shows the radius of curvature a increasing from zero at proper time $-\tau_0$ on up to its maximum value of a_0 at $\tau = 0$. If nothing intervened, the sphere would continue on to the right side of the curve, collapsing to a singularity at proper time $+\tau_0$. Thus the sphere would start as a white hole and end as a black hole.

Klein calculated the Schwarzschild time t it would take for a sphere of dust to collapse from its maximum radius of curvature a_0 (at a Schwarzschild time defined as $t = 0$) to some smaller radius of curvature a. I have recalculated his expression for the reverse situation to get the time t it would take the dust sphere to expand from a radius of curvature a out to the maximum radius of curvature a_o. I have kept Klein's definition of $t = 0$ as being the time that the radius of curvature reaches its maximum, so all times before that instant are negative. Modifying Klein's nomenclature a bit, I get the following expression [equation (20)] for the Schwarzschild time:

$$t = -t_o \left[\frac{b^3}{1 + b^2} \log\left(\frac{\zeta + b}{\zeta - b}\right) + \frac{\zeta}{1 - \zeta^2} + \left(\frac{1 + 3 b^2}{1 + b^2}\right)\left(\frac{\pi}{2} - \text{Arctan } \zeta\right) \right]$$

The parameters t_o, ζ, and b in the above equation are defined as follows [equations (21a,b,c)]:

$$t_o \equiv \frac{a_o}{c\sqrt{1 - \eta_o^2}}, \quad \zeta \equiv \sqrt{\frac{a_o}{a_o - a}}\sqrt{\frac{1 - \eta_o^2}{1 - \eta^2}} - 1, \quad b \equiv \frac{\eta_o}{\sqrt{1 - \eta_o^2}}$$

The normalizing parameter t_o is a constant, has units of time, and is greater than the time it would take light to travel a distance a_o. The parameter ζ is a dimensionless variable which gets larger as the radius of curvature a increases with proper time. The parameter b is a constant. Just to refresh your memory, η is the co-moving radial coordinate and is r/a; η_o is the value of η for the edge of the matter, namely r_o/a. Figure 10 plots eq. (20) with the matter radius set at $\eta_o = 0.5$.

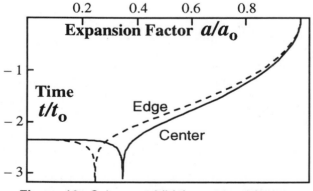

Figure 10. Schwarzschild time at two places.

The solid curve shows the real part of the normalized Schwarz-schild time t/t_0 at the center of the universe, that is, for $\eta = 0$. The dashed curve shows t/t_0 at the edge of the matter sphere, that is, for $\eta = \eta_0 = 0.5$. Notice that as the expansion factor a/a_0 increases to roughly the value 0.25, the dashed curve goes to minus infinity and then returns, just as the curve in Figure 7. This marks the point in the expansion when the event horizon reaches the edge. A little later in the expansion, at $a/a_0 = 0.35$, when the event horizon reaches the center, the solid curve also goes to minus infinity and returns. Inside the event horizon the Schwarz-schild time also has a relatively small but non-zero imaginary component. The interpretation of an imaginary interval in section 3 (as spacelike rather than timelike) suggests that this imaginary part contributes to the stretching of space inside the event horizon.

Although the dashed and solid curves coincide at the beginning and end of the expansion, they are considerably different in between. The dashed line goes to minus infinity at a smaller value of a/a_0 than the solid line does because the event horizon reaches the edge of the matter sooner than it reaches the center.

After the event horizon reaches the center, the dashed curve is significantly above the solid curve until the end of the expansion. The difference between these two lines represents a large difference in Schwarzschild age. During much of the expansion, the outer parts of the universe would be older than the inner parts. At a given stage in the expansion, the age difference would be proportional to the distance from the center.

Figure 11 (next page) shows how the difference in age, $t(\eta) - t(0)$, depends on the proper distance (see Figure 8). The values used in this figure are all consistent with $r_0 = 20$ billion light-years, $\eta_0 = 0.5$, and $a/a_0 = 0.4$: $a_0 = 40$ billion light-years, $t_0 = 46.2$ billion years, and $a = 16$ billion light-years. The curve has different shapes at other expansion factors, but the overall age increase to billions of years at large distances exists during most of the expansion after the event horizon reaches earth.

Except very near the event horizon, the speed of light as measured in Schwarzschild coordinates is close to c, so these large Schwarzschild ages allow time for light to cover most, if not

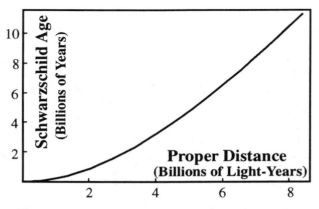

Figure 11. Age versus distance from the earth.

all, the great distances to get to us during the expansion. If the expansion can take place within six days of proper time as measured on earth, then we have at least an approximate solution to the problem of seeing galaxies while standing on a young earth. Eq. (19b) shows that when the cosmological constant Λ is zero, the expansion is very slow. However, cosmologists have long known that large values of Λ, corresponding to a large tension applied to space, will enormously accelerate the expansion [32]. As I pointed out in Section 5, there is no physical law preventing an expansion much faster than the speed of light. What we really need to be specific at this point is the generalized form of equations (17) through (21) for non-zero Λ. I have made good progress on this purely mathematical problem, but as of May 30, 1994, I have not had time to complete it. The equations of this section are not a specific solution, but they imply that a solution exists, and they offer a rough outline of its basic features. Thus I think we have the main features of an answer to the light transit time problem.

14. RED SHIFTS AND THE COSMIC MICROWAVE BACKGROUND

Many authors show how the Robertson-Walker metric, eq. (5), leads to a red shift in the wavelength of electromagnetic radiation as the universe expands [48, pp. 415-418]. Since the same metric applies to our bounded cosmos with center-oriented coordinates (see beginning paragraphs of previous section), we can use the same result to specify the red shift as seen from the center:

$$\frac{\lambda_2}{\lambda_1} = \frac{a_2}{a_1} \qquad (22)$$

Here λ_1 and λ_2 are, respectively, the wavelengths of the light at emission and reception; a_1 and a_2 are, respectively, the radii of curvature of the cosmos at emission and reception. Often astronomers specify red shifts in terms of a dimensionless parameter z, which is defined as $(\lambda_2 - \lambda_1)/\lambda_1$, changing eq. (22) to the form:

$$z = \frac{a_2}{a_1} - 1 \qquad (23)$$

I have also derived these results from Klein's metric, eq. (16). In an expanding cosmos, a_2 is greater than a_1, so λ_2 is greater than λ_1 and the red shift parameter z is positive. Notice that these equations do not depend on velocity at all, so the effect cannot be a Doppler shift, as I explained in Section 5. Instead the effect is entirely due to the change of the radius of curvature of space while the photons are *in transit*. If you think of light as waves traveling on a sheet of rubber, these equations say that, as the sheet is stretched out, the wavelengths stretch out along with it. The equations say that the rate of expansion has nothing to do with the amount of red shift, which depends only on the initial and final values of a. As far as the red shifts are concerned, it does not matter whether the expansion took place in 20 billion years or six days.

In 1929, Edwin Hubble found that the red shifts of light from galaxies are approximately proportional to their distance r [26]:

$$z \approx \frac{H}{c} r \qquad (24)$$

As I mentioned in section 1, there are exceptions to this, but the trend is very clear. The parameter H is called the *Hubble constant*. At present, astronomers cannot measure great distances to better than a factor of two, so they do not know the Hubble constant to better than that accuracy. But whatever the exact distances are, the cosmology I am outlining here asserts that the galaxies were indeed at those great distances when the light they emitted began its journey to us. It also asserts that the amount of expansion occurring between emission and reception was roughly the same as the standard theory claims. Thus, without doing any detailed calculations, we can say that the value of the Hubble constant given by this theory should be about the same as observed.

We now come to the third item on my list of large-scale phenomena to be explained, the cosmic microwave background radiation. Various authors have shown [49, p. 533, eq. (15.6.17)] the following: if space is filled with thermal radiation corresponding to a temperature T_1 when it has a radius of curvature a_1, then when space expands to a radius of curvature a_2, the same stretching effect which caused the red shift of light waves will also red-shift the heat waves. That drops the thermal radiation temperature to a value T_2 given by:

$$\frac{T_2}{T_1} = \frac{a_1}{a_2} \qquad (25)$$

Thus, if the early cosmos was filled with thermal radiation of high temperature and uniformity, then the expansion of a bounded cosmos would have the same kind of low-temperature microwave background we observe today. The next section shows that such radiation in the early cosmos would be a very reasonable result of the Genesis account.

15. RECONSTRUCTION OF SOME CREATION EVENTS
Now let's use our imaginations and try to reconstruct some of the events of the creation week from both the biblical and scientific information. At some points I will have to speculate in order to provide specific details, so please regard this reconstruction as a tentative outline of events, subject to radical revision as we learn more.

In Appendix B (section 8) I show evidence that in the first instant of creation the "deep" consisted of ordinary liquid water at normal density and temperature. This requires the existence of functioning water molecules with their constituent atoms, electrons and nuclei; in turn that requires electromagnetic and nuclear forces to be in operation. These forces (especially electromagnetism) are deeply enmeshed with relativity, and so their existence implies that relativity was operating at this time. There is also biblical evidence that gravity was operating at that instant, and if it were very strong, there would be a clearly-defined interface between the water and the presumed vacuum above it. Gravity would also shape the water into a sphere. There is biblical evidence that the sphere was slowly rotating with respect to the space within which it existed. There was no visible light at the surface of the sphere.

To contain all the mass of the visible universe, equations (8) and (12) say that the sphere of water would have an initial radius of at least *one light-year*. (Actually the size would have to be greater than that to account for the mass of the "waters above the heavens," but that mass is unknown.) One light-year is surprisingly small compared to the present cosmos, but it is still large enough to justify the biblical name of the sphere, "the deep." The sphere would be well within its event horizon, which according to eq. (14) would be 450 million light-years further out. Thus the universe started as either a black hole or white hole. I suggest here that it was a black hole, and that God let gravity take its course. The physics of black holes (section 11) do not permit matter in a black hole to remain motionless; it must fall inward. So unless God intervened, the sphere would collapse inward. The fall would be faster than the speed of light, as measured in Schwarzschild coordinates (remember the great speed of the astronaut as he approached point C in Fig. 6).

As the radius of the sphere shrank, the temperature, pressure, and density would rise to enormous values. Descending into the interior, we would find a depth at which molecules would be dissociated and atoms would be ionized. Further down, nuclei would be torn apart into neutrons and protons. Yet further down, even elementary particles would be ripped apart, making a dense plasma of gluons and quarks.

At a certain range of depths, thermonuclear fusion reactions would begin, forming heavier nuclei from lighter ones (nucleosynthesis) and liberating huge amounts of energy. An intense light would illuminate the interior. As the compression continued, the fusion reactions would reach a shallow enough depth to allow light to reach the surface, thus ending the darkness at that level. The strong gravity would cause light leaving the surface to return to it, so light at the surface would be coming from all sides. The sphere would have no dark side.

As the compression continued, the gravity would became so strong that light could no longer reach the surface, thus re-darkening it. Appendix B (section 13) offers biblical evidence that the Spirit of God became a localized light source, giving the sphere a bright side and a dark side.

Meanwhile, conservation of angular momentum would have caused the sphere to speed up its rotation as the collapse proceeded. To be consistent with the Genesis account, the surface would execute a full rotation between the beginning and the end of day one. When the rotation of the sphere reached relativistically significant speeds, the Schwarzschild metric would no longer be an accurate description of the vacuum outside the sphere. Instead the more complex Kerr metric [24, pp. 161-168] would have to be used, and I haven't taken on that problem yet. As yet there is no known exact metric for the conditions inside the sphere at this point. However, because (as measured in Schwarzschild coordinates) the distance is about a light-year and the velocity of collapse is greater than c, we can say that the collapse would take less than a year of Schwarzschild time. Proper time as measured at the surface of the sphere would be less than the Schwarzschild time, and I suspect that it amounted to an ordinary day.

At some point the black hole had to become a white hole. I propose that God did this on day two by increasing the cosmological "constant" Λ to a large positive value, beginning a rapid, inflationary expansion of space. He marked off a large volume within the ball wherein material would be allowed to pull apart into fragments and clusters as it expanded, but He required the "waters below" and the "waters above" to stay coherently together, as Figure 12(a) on the next page illustrates.

Cooling would proceed as rapidly as the expansion. Visible matter would cool directly by expansion, and also by losing heat to the material of space itself, according to general relativity [40, pp. 344, 355-356] [36]. Matter above and below the expanse would expand but stay dense. Matter in the expanse would be drawn apart into clusters of hydrogen and helium plasma. Figure 12(b) illustrates this phase of the expansion. At some point in the expansion, when the radius of curvature a was about a thousand times smaller than today's value, the plasma in the expanse would cool to about 3000 Kelvin, at which point the plasma would begin forming atoms and the expanse would become transparent.

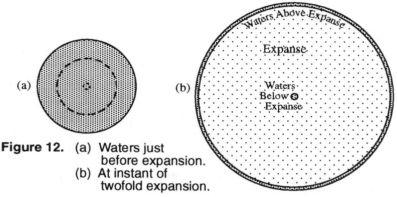

Figure 12. (a) Waters just before expansion.
(b) At instant of twofold expansion.

At this point, thermal radiation in the expanse would be very uniform and have a blackbody spectrum, having been surrounded by optically thick walls above and below during the previous stage of expansion. According to eq. (25), the radiation temperature would now begin dropping from 3000 Kelvin to much lower values, in direct proportion to the increase in the radius of curvature a. At the end of the expansion, the radiation temperature would have dropped to the 2.74 Kelvin we see today. This explanation of the cosmic microwave background is not too different from that provided by the big bang theories, except for the boundedness and the optically thick "walls" around the expanse.

16. DAYS THREE TO SIX

The inflationary expansion of space could possibly have had second-order effects on nuclear forces and on the transport of heat from hot matter to the material of space itself [40, pp. 344, 355-356] [36]. If so, such mechanisms could explain the evidence for both rapid radioactive decay and rapid volume cooling which creationists have lately begun to notice. God could have used radioactive decay on the third day to heat the continental cratons (which today contain most of the earth's radioactive nuclei) and provide power for other geologic work, followed by volume

125

cooling to solidify batholiths and the asthenosphere. The thermal expansion of the supercontinent would make it more buoyant with respect to the mantle rock, lifting the continent above the waters and causing them to gather in the ocean basins.

At some time during the expansion, probably on the third day, the waters above the heavens would reach the event horizon and pass beyond it. After that the event horizon would begin rapidly shrinking toward the earth. At the same time, gravity would be drawing together the atoms of hydrogen, helium, and other elements in each cluster left behind by the expansion. There would be plenty of Schwarzschild time for that process.

I suggest that the event horizon reached earth early in the morning of the fourth day. During that day of proper time on earth, according to my theory, billions of years worth of physical processes took place in the distant cosmos. I also suggest that early in the fourth morning, God finished coalescing the clusters of material left behind in the expansion and allowed thermonuclear fusion to ignite in the newly-formed stars. At this point, the stars would find themselves clustered into galaxies. As with other things in the Genesis account, the formation of stars, solar system(s?), and galaxies would be caused by a combination of natural events and direct action by God. At this point I am not trying to be specific as to which was which. During the fourth day the distant stars aged billions of years, while their light also had that much time to travel here. While the light from the most distant galaxy we have seen was traveling to us, the universe expanded by about a factor of five, stretching the light's wavelength by the same factor and giving it a red-shift parameter of about four [see eq. (23)].

Appendix B (section 7) gives reasons to think that God stopped the expansion, reducing Λ to a small positive value or zero, before the evening of the sixth day. (Appendix B, section 7, also points out some evidence for another episode of expansion during the Genesis flood.) Thus Adam and Eve, gazing up for the first time into the new night sky, would be able to see the Milky Way, the Andromeda galaxy, and all the other splendors in the heavens that declare the glory of God.

17. CONCLUSION

Jean-Pierre Luminet [30, p. 161] quotes Dennis Sutton as writing that "the frontiers of science are always a bizarre mixture of new truth, reasonable hypothesis, and wild conjecture." By those criteria, then, you will probably agree that this paper is on the "frontiers of science" — or perhaps beyond! But I want to remind you that the essential hypothesis of this paper, that matter in the universe is bounded, is quite reasonable. After all, every other created thing we know of has limits, so why should we expect even the biggest thing God created to be any different?

Furthermore, the hypothesis is not something I concocted myself to generate an *ad hoc* explanation for the cosmological difficulties of young-earth creationism. Instead the idea of a bounded universe flows very naturally from the central idea of young-earth creationism: that the Bible is to be taken straightforwardly.

If the universe is bounded, the main points of this cosmology follow quite scientifically from the amount of visible matter in the universe, the evidence for its expansion, and the experimentally well-established general theory of relativity. The logical conclusion is that the universe began its existence in a black hole or a white hole. The phenomena surrounding black holes seem strange to us mainly because we are unfamiliar with them, not because they are impossible. At any rate, I did not invent the idea of such phenomena. The only thing I have done is apply the same ideas to the universe as a whole and explore some of the consequences.

At this point, I consider this paper only the outlines of a theory. As such it furnishes us with qualitative answers to the major cosmological phenomena I listed in the introduction, but it is not yet well enough developed to make detailed quantitative predictions which would observationally distinguish it from conventional theories. A large amount of work needs to be done to bring it to that point, far more than I can do alone, so I invite other creationist scientists and students to join me in this work.

There is a good possibility that developments of this theory can explain many of the anomalies encountered by the conventional theories, such as superluminal quasar jets [10], proportions of nuclei found in the cosmos [18], vestiges of rotation in the cosmos

[37], numbers of galaxies at large red shifts [6], the extraordinary uniformity of the cosmic microwave background [38], the extreme brightness of the universe (10^9 photons per nucleon) [27], the cosmological constant problem [49], the flatness problem [43], and so forth.

In particular, the "quantized" distribution of galactic red shifts [3] [22], observed by various astronomers with increasing certainty over the last few decades, seems to contradict the Copernican principle and all cosmologies founded on it — including the big bang. But the effect seems to have a ready explanation in terms of my new non-Copernican "white hole" cosmology.

This paper covers a great deal of scientific territory unfamiliar to many readers. But the bottom line is simple: God used relativity to make a young universe.

ACKNOWLEDGMENTS
A number of people have helped me greatly in this work. Roy Holt asked a question that made me realize the importance of the Copernican principle. John Baumgardner has encouraged me and helped untangle my thinking. James Dritt has given sensible advice and been a good editor. Gerald Schroeder's ideas [44], referred to in section 9, though not quite correct, may have helped me solidify mine. Barry Setterfield's theory, while not correct in my eventual opinion, was a great stimulus to me. A creationist astrophysics graduate student at a major university has helped me on several mathematical problems. Many other creationist friends have prayed for this project. My heartfelt thanks go to all these people.

REFERENCES

[1]   R. Akridge, T. Barnes, and H. S. Slusher, **A recent creation explanation of the 3° K background black body radiation**, *Creation Research Society Quarterly* **18:3** (1981) 159-162.

[2]   G. R. Akridge, **The universe is bigger than 15.71 light years**, *Creation Research Society Quarterly* **21:1** (1984) 18-22.

[3]   Anonymous, **Quantized redshifts: what's going on here?** *Sky and Telescope* (August 1992) 28-29.

[4]   G. D. Birkoff, *Relativity and Modern Physics*, 1923, Harvard University Press, Cambridge, Mass.

[5]   H. Bondi, *Cosmology*, 1960, Cambridge University Press, London.

[6]   T. J. Broadhurst, R. S. Ellis, and K. Glazebrook, **Faint galaxies: evolution and cosmological curvature**, *Nature* **355** (2 January 1992) 55-58.

[7]   J. Byl, **On small curved-space models of the universe**, *Creation Research Society Quarterly* **25:3** (1988) 138-140.

[8]   E. F. Chaffin, **A determination of the speed of light in the seventeenth century**, *Creation Research Society Quarterly* **29:3** (1992) 115-120.

[9]   K. C. Chambers, G. K. Miley, and W. J. M. van Breugel, **4C 41.17: a radio galaxy at a red-shift of 3.8**, *Astrophysical Journal* **363:1** (1990) 21-39.

[10]   R. J. Davis, S. C. Unwin, and T. W. B. Muxlow, **Large-scale superluminal motion in the quasar 3C273**, *Nature* **354** (5 December 1991) 374-376.

[11]   D. B. DeYoung, *Questions and Answers on Astronomy and the Bible*, 1989, Baker Book House, Grand Rapids.

[12]   A. Einstein, **Cosmological considerations on the general theory of relativity**, *The Principle of Relativity*, 1952, Dover Publications, New York, 177-188. Translated from **Kosmologische Betrachtungen zur allgemeinen Relativitätstheorie**, *Sitzungsberichte der Preussischen Akad. d. Wissenschaften* (1917) 142-152.

[13]   A. Einstein, **The foundations of the general theory of relativity**, in *The Principle of Relativity,* 1952, Dover Publications, New York, 111-164. Translated from **Die**

Grundlage der allgemeinen Relativitätstheorie, *Annalen der Physik* **49** (1916) 769.

[14]   A. Einstein, *The Meaning of Relativity*, 1956, Fifth Edition, Princeton University Press, Princeton.

[15]   A. Einstein, **Ether and the theory of relativity**, in *Sidelights on Relativity*, 1983, Dover Publications, New York, 1-25. Translated from an address delivered on May 5, 1920 at the University of Leyden.

[16]   M. G. Evered, **The recent decrease in the velocity of light — what decrease?**, *Creation Ex Nihilo Technical Journal* **7:1** (1993) 93-102.

[17]   T. Ferris, **Needed: a better name for the big bang**, *Sky & Telescope* **86:2** (1993) 4-5.

[18]   F. Flam, **In the beginning, let there be beryllium**, *Science* **255** (10 January 1992) 162-163.

[19]   T. Frankel, *Gravitational Curvature: An Introduction to Einstein's Theory*, 1979, W. H. Freeman and Company, San Francisco.

[20]   J. R. Gott, **Implications of the Copernican principle for our future prospects**, *Nature* **363** (27 May 1993) 315-319.

[21]   A. H. Guth, **Inflationary universe: a possible solution to the horizon and flatness problems**, *Physical Review* **D 23:2** (1981) 347-356.

[22]   B. N. G. Guthrie and W. M. Napier, **Evidence for redshift periodicity in nearby field galaxies**, *Monthly Notices of the Royal Astronomical Society* **253** (1991) 533-544.

[23]   E. R. Harrison, *Cosmology: The Science of the Universe,* 1981, Cambridge University Press, Cambridge.

[24]   S. W. Hawking and G. F. R. Ellis, *The Large Scale Structure of Space-Time*, 1973, Cambridge University Press, Cambridge.

[25] S. W. Hawking, *A Brief History of Time*, 1988, Bantam Books, New York.

[26] E. Hubble, **A relation between distance and radial velocity among extra-galactic nebulae**, *Proceedings of the National Academy of Science* **15** (1929) 168-173.

[27] D. W. Hughes, **Considering cosmology**, *Nature* **353** (31 October 1991) 804-805.

[28] O. Klein, **Einige probleme der allgemeinen relativitätstheorie**, in *Werner Heinsenberg und die Physik unserer Zeit*, Fritz Bopp, Editor, 1961, Friedr. Vieweg & Sohn, Braunschweig, 58-72. In German. Partial translation, **Several problems of the theory of general relativity**, 13 pages, available from D. R. Humphreys, address on first page of this paper. Send $2.00 for cost of copying plus postage.

[29] L. D. Landau and E. M. Lifshitz, *The Classical Theory of Fields*, 1975, Fourth Revised English Edition, Pergamon Press, Oxford.

[30] J-P. Luminet, *Black Holes*, 1992, Cambridge University Press, Cambridge.

[31] C. W. Misner, K. S. Thorne, and J. A. Wheeler, *Gravitation*, 1973, W. H. Freeman and Company, New York.

[32] M. Moles, **Physically permitted cosmological models with nonzero cosmological constant**, *Astrophysical Journal* **382** (December 1 1991) 369-376.

[33] P. Moon and D. E. Spencer, **Binary stars and the velocity of light**, *Journal of the Optical Society of America* **43:8** (1953) 635-641.

[34] J. V. Narlikar, *Introduction to Cosmology*, 983, Jones and Bartlett Publishers, Boston.

[35] T. Norman and B. Setterfield, *The Atomic Constants, Light, and Time*, 1987, Technical Monograph, Flinders University, Adelaide, Australia.

[36] J. Pachner, **Nonconservation of energy during cosmic evolution**, *Physical Review Letters* **12:4** (1964) 117-118.

[37] V. F. Panov and Yu. G. Sbytov, **Accounting for Birch's observed anisotropy of the universe: cosmological rotation?**, *Soviet Physics JETP* **74:3** (1992) 411-415.

[38] R. B. Partridge, **The seeds of cosmic structure**, *Science* **257** (10 July 1992) 178-179.

[39] W. Rindler, *Essential Relativity*, 1977, Revised Second Edition, Springer-Verlag, New York.

[40] H. P. Robertson and T. W. Noonan, *Relativity and Cosmology*, 1968, W. B. Saunders Company, Philadelphia.

[41] R. Rucker, *The Fourth Dimension*, 1984, Houghton Miflin Company, Boston.

[42] C. Sagan, *Cosmos*, 1980, Random House, New York.

[43] P. Scheuer, **Weighing the universe**, *Nature* **361** (14 January 1993) 112.

[44] G. L. Schroeder, **The universe — 6 days and 13 billion years old**, *Jerusalem Post*, September 7, 1991. Schroeder's "6 days" is at the "edge of the universe," while his "13 billion years" is on the earth — exactly the reverse of what I am saying! A letter from Dr. Schroeder (10/29/93) indicates his cosmological ideas are quite different from the one I am presenting here.

[45] B. F. Schutz, *A First Course in General Relativity*, 1985, Cambridge University Press, Cambridge.

[46] R. Sexl and H. Sexl, *White Dwarfs—Black Holes*, 1979, Academic Press, New York.

[47] P. M. Steidl, *The Earth, the Stars, and the Bible*, 1979, Baker Book House, Grand Rapids.

[48] S. Weinberg, *Gravitation and Cosmology*, 1972, John Wiley & Sons, New York.

[49] S. Weinberg, **The cosmological constant problem**, *Reviews of Modern Physics* **61:1** (1989) 1-23.

[50] S. Weinberg, *Dreams of a Final Theory*, 1992, Pantheon Books, New York.

[51] J. C. Whitcomb, Jr., and H. M. Morris, *The Genesis Flood*, 1961, Baker Book House, Grand Rapids.

INDEX

Quantity Discounts

Below are the numbers and amounts for ordering *Starlight and Time* in quantities over 11 books.

12-23	**5.25** *each*
24-35	**4.95** *each*
36 or more	**4.50** *each*

To order quantity discounts contact:

Master Books
P.O. Box 26060
Colorado Springs, CO 80936 U.S.A.
(719) 591-0800

Toll free in the U.S.A.
1-800-999-3777

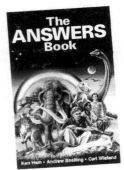